In Praise of
DEADLOCK

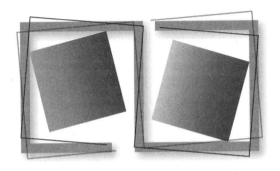

In Praise of
DEADLOCK

How Partisan Struggle
Makes Better Laws

W. Lee Rawls

Woodrow Wilson Center Press
Washington, D.C.

The Johns Hopkins University Press
Baltimore

EDITORIAL OFFICES
Woodrow Wilson Center Press
One Woodrow Wilson Plaza
1300 Pennsylvania Avenue, N.W.
Washington, D.C. 20004-3027
Telephone: 202-691-4029
www.wilsoncenter.org

ORDER FROM
The Johns Hopkins University Press
Hampden Station
P.O. Box 50370
Baltimore, Maryland 21211
Telephone: 1-800-537-5487
www.press.jhu.edu/books/

Library of Congress Cataloging-in-Publication Data

Rawls, W. Lee.
    In praise of deadlock : how partisan struggle makes
better laws / W. Lee Rawls.
        p.   cm.
    Includes bibliographical references and index.
    ISBN 978-0-8018-9404-6 (hardcover : alk. paper)—
ISBN 978-0-8018-9403-9 (pbk. : alk. paper)
    1. United States. Congress. Senate—Freedom of
debate. 2. Filibusters (Political science)—United States.
3. Legislation—United States—History. 4. Parliamentary
practice—United States. 5. United States. Congress—
Rules and practice. I. Title.
    JK1161.R38   2009
    328.73′077—dc22

                                        2009012003

Woodrow Wilson International Center for Scholars

The Woodrow Wilson International Center for Scholars, established by Congress in 1968 and headquartered in Washington, D.C., is the living, national memorial to President Wilson.

The Center is a nonpartisan institution of advanced research, supported by public and private funds, engaged in the study of national and world affairs. The Center establishes and maintains a neutral forum for free, open, and informed dialogue.

The Center's mission is to commemorate the ideals and concerns of Woodrow Wilson by providing a link between the world of ideas and the world of policy, by bringing a broad spectrum of individuals together to discuss important public policy issues, by serving to bridge cultures and viewpoints, and by seeking to find common ground.

Conclusions or opinions expressed in Center publications and programs are those of the authors and speakers and do not necessarily reflect the views of the Center staff, fellows, trustees, advisory groups, or any individuals or organizations that provide financial support to the Center.

The Center is the publisher of The Wilson Quarterly and home of Woodrow Wilson Center Press, dialogue radio and television, and the monthly newsletter "Centerpoint." For more information about the Center's activities and publications, please visit us on the web at www.wilsoncenter.org.

Lee H. Hamilton, President and Director

"Dedicated to the One I Love"
—The Shirelles, 1961

Contents

Tables and Figures

Tables

Figures

In Praise of
DEADLOCK

 INTRODUCTION

The American Legislative Process—For Adults Only

> The only good history books are those written by the people
> who shaped the events themselves, or were involved in shap-
> ing them; or at least had the luck to shape similar ones.
> —Michel de Montaigne[1]

The Consensus View

In 1950, the American Political Science Association
wrote a report called "Toward a More Responsible Two-
Party System" that criticized the American political system for its "sluggish," "indifferent" pursuit of political
consensus. It then urged a revitalization of the two-party
system that would offer the electorate clear policy choices
while holding its elected representatives accountable.

The conclusions of this 1950 report were echoed in a
series of books in the 1960s whose titles speak for them-

selves: *The Deadlock of Democracy* (1963), *Obstacle Course on Capitol Hill* (1964), *Congress in Crisis* (1966), and the most inspired title of the group, *Congress: The Sapless Branch* (1964).[2] The most famous of these was *The Deadlock of Democracy,* written by the historian James McGregor Burns. For Burns, the Madisonian system of checks and balances in the Constitution had become a "political system that evades and confuses the real issues rather than sharpening and resolving them."[3] For Burns, the solution lay in two national parties with the winner adopting Jefferson's preference for strong majority rule, advancing a coherent national agenda.[4]

Forty-five years later, with their dream of a vibrant two-party system realized, academic and journalistic observers are having buyers' remorse. Again, a wave of books with self-explanatory titles has broken upon us. *The Broken Branch* (2006), *The Second Civil War* (2007), *Party Wars* (2006), *Polarized America* (2006), *Stalemate* (2003), and my favorite, *Fight Club Politics* (2006), have all appeared, decrying the threat posed to American democracy by the "toxic," "polarized," "hyperpartisanship" of the modern two-party system.[5] The final irony is that many of these modern-day political Jeremiahs urge the return to the lost paradise of civility and bipartisanship found in the 1950s and early 1960s, exactly the era trashed by their academic and journalistic predecessors.

Listing these titles presents an entertaining but obvious oversimplification of the debate on the role of parties and quality of the American legislative process.[6] Nevertheless, the view that the American legislative process is hopelessly partisan and dysfunctional is received popular wisdom and was the centerpiece of the 2008 presidential campaign, with Barack Obama prevailing as the superior agent of change. In the immediate aftermath of Obama's victory, millennial sentiments of the "hope that the era of racial backlash and wedge politics is over" abounded.[7] David Broder of the *Washington Post,* the dean of political columnists in America, and a steadfast proponent of "bipartisanship," urged that America move "beyond partisan gridlock," going as far as to endorse the "wisdom" of seeking "85-vote majorities" in the Senate.[8]

In the aftermath of President Obama's victory in enacting a $787 billion economic stimulus bill in mid-February 2009—as this study was receiving its final edits—there was considerable journalistic angst over the loss of these high hopes for a new era of bipartisanship. Because the bill passed without any Republican votes in the House, and with only three Republican votes in the Senate, the editorial page of the *New York Times* chided the Obama team for its "futile pursuit of bipartisanship," while the *Washington Post*'s Dana Milbank announced the dawn of a new era of "post-post-partisanship."[9]

The Practitioner's Response

The political practitioners of the legislative process— who, in contrast to their manic-depressive journalistic colleagues, found the general course of the Obama stimulus package predictable—have been relatively silent in print. There have been occasional interviews of former congressional leaders and the printing of their memoirs. Political consultants, with only peripheral legislative experience, are teeming on the nightly news shows. But there has been little effort by those with experience to put their thoughts in writing. Two exceptions are Don Wolfensberger's *Congress and the People* and John Hilley's *The Challenge of Legislation*.[10] Wolfensberger, the staff director for the House of Representatives' Rules Committee during the 1990s, published his insightful study on the quality of the congressional deliberative process in 2000, before the recent "hyperpartisanship" literary surge.

In contrast, Hilley, President Bill Clinton's director of legislative affairs, published his analysis of the 1997 balanced budget legislation in 2008. As such, it is timely, and on point. Moreover, it is the best treatment of a complex piece of legislation in the modern era.[11] Throughout, it has the ring of truth for any practitioner who has labored through the Hades of a heavily contested, complex piece of legislation. Also, parts of it present a direct refutation to the millennial bipartisan school of thought that has dominated since the 2008 presidential election. Hilley does this by stating the obvious:

> At the base of our democratic system of government is a competition for elective office; political competition among partisans is how we Americans pick winners and losers and empower the winners to make big decisions. Winning elections is the essential precondition for exercising government's considerable powers.[12]

Hilley then goes on to make a philosophical point that strikes directly at the lamentations of the "hyperpartisan" school of critics:

> Partisan competition has been at the center of our struggle to advance as a people and as a nation. It has been our most important engine for adaptation and change— one that remains in full motion.[13]

In short, the "constructive tension" of political competition is the source of strength and energy in American democracy. Competition is good for us.[14] This is not a novel idea. Not just America, but Western civilization as well, has adopted competitive systems for overall collective benefits in a variety of situations. The most obvious two are the use of competitive markets in capitalism and the employment of a system of adversarial advocacy in our courts.[15] These competitive systems are hard on the participants, and grim to watch. But from these competitive frameworks, we derive economic growth and a judicial system dedicated to justice. Hilley is not the first, just the most recent, proponent of the value of competition in our political system.

Most of the evidence of the critics on the state of the American political system is anecdotal. The "hyperpartisan" critique with its "millennial bipartisan" solution is filled with tales of rudeness between members of Congress in the heat of combat. There is also a good dosage of entertaining tales of procedural "dirty tricks," defended in turn as necessary "hardball" by the perpetrators. Despite their entertainment value, this anecdote-based approach is flawed—dangerously so. The most serious flaw of this approach is the lack of any structural analysis on how the legislative process actually works. Thus, individual anecdotes are used to cast a pall over the entire legislative process. Not only does this approach give an inaccurate description of the strengths and weaknesses of the American legislative process; it also does not offer sound guidance as to what parts of the process need to be saved and what parts need to be changed.

This study takes a different approach. As a fellow practitioner with Wolfensberger and Hilley, it is the result of my thirty-eight years in Washington participating in the legislative process. Along the way, I have been the chief of staff to Senator Pete Domenici (R-N.M.) and Senator Bill Frist (R-Tenn.). My time in the Senate also included a stint as Senator Frist's chief of staff when he was majority leader. Leadership positions in the House and Senate, whether on the majority or minority side, offer a unique vantage point. The entire two-year period of a session of Congress, with its many subplots, is a single drama all leading up to elections, when your efforts are either vindicated or rejected by the American electorate. Legislative practitioners speak a common language and hold many common views. It is this common perspective of legislative practitioners from both sides of the political aisle that I hope to bring to the debate over the nature of the American legislative machine and how well it is functioning for American democracy.

In addition to my time as chief of staff to the Senate majority leadership, I have opened two Washington law firms, where I engaged in the usual Washington lawyer chores of lobbying and fund-raising. I have also spent time in the executive branch, first as assistant attorney general for legislative affairs under George H. W. Bush and more recently as chief of staff to the director of the Federal Bureau of Investigation. It should be no surprise that someone with so many battle scars from the legislative arena would have strong views.

These views have been fleshed out in fifteen years of teaching as an adjunct professor at the College of William and Mary. The process of turning the intuitive judgments and gut instincts of over three decades of legislative experience into course materials has forced me to add structure and coherence to my views. Answering the pointed questions of the young has also forced me to take a more systematic view of the legislative process. In particular, I have felt for a long time that it is important to take a step back and evaluate the modern American legislative process as a whole. Using a systemwide lens that examines each of the parts and their interactions allows for an overall net judgment on the virtues and defects of the legislative process that the popular anecdotal approaches cannot provide.[16]

This approach has the virtue of sparing the reader a point-by-point response to every anecdote or critique employed by the "hyperpartisan" school.[17] Moreover, once we have established an overall view of the legislative system, the validity of many of the points of contention can be quickly sorted out. Some of the criticisms of the legislative process are easily dismissed. Others are on point and require discussion.

Human Nature

Salted throughout the discussion will be a targeted discussion of the interaction of human nature and the legislative process. For years, such a discussion would have been off limits. For most of the twentieth century, social science orthodoxy had walled off human culture from human biology. Any transgressions were violently attacked.

All this has changed. Ever since Noam Chomsky figured out that humans are born with, or "hard-wired" for, the ability to speak languages, and that the specific language spoken by an individual is a function of her particular culture, the science of "human nature" has broken through the old taboos. Today, the cognitive sciences, evolutionary biology, psychology, the neurosciences, and anthropology have converged to produce an impressive body of support for the "psychic unity of humankind" that transcends culture.[18]

The above should trigger at least two alarms. The notion of a hands-on political practitioner wandering through the intellectual minefield of human nature should set off the first alarm. Second, discussions of human nature often have been employed by political ideologues to support the view of a flawed humanity in perpetual conflict that must be subjected to a high level of coercion to maintain civilization.

On the first count, I will use the new insights on human nature on only several narrow issues. But the explanatory power of this new evidence is valuable in explaining several issues that commentators have ascribed to individual, partisan, or moral failings, when in fact the participants in the legislative process are just being human. This also has been happening in economics, where the founders of prospect theory, Amos Tversky and Daniel Kahneman (the latter won a Nobel prize), have provided insights on the limitations of the human mind in assessing risk, particularly future risk. Some political scientists are also following suit, with scholars such as John Hibbing at the University of Nebraska abandoning traditional approaches to examine the genetic basis of political preferences.[19]

On the second count, the news from the intellectual front on the science of human nature is surprisingly positive. Humans are genetically coded not only to compete but also, under certain circumstances, to cooperate. They not only generate conflict but also resolve conflicts. And perhaps most surprising, they have an inborn sense of morality that tells them what is fair.[20] The fact that "altruism, compassion, empathy, love, conscience and a sense of justice . . . have a firm genetic basis" should put to rest the fear of any latent ideological agenda in the study of human nature.[21]

In her book *Party Wars*, Barbara Sinclair accurately describes the United States Senate as a "peculiar combination of conflict and cooperation, of aggressive exploitation of the rules and of accommodation."[22] Her description neatly matches that of Aristotle's "political animal" provided by the new science of human nature.

Some Contrarian Conclusions

This description of the Senate also provides a segue into the study's conclusions. Despite the many moving parts of the legislative process, there is one in particular worth focusing on: the filibuster in the Senate. The other major pieces of the legislative process, the House of Representatives and the president with his veto, are comparatively straightforward in operation and effect. As we will see, they are not without controversy, but they are invariably predictable.

The filibuster is different. It turns the Senate into a body that requires a supermajority of 60 out of 100 votes to pass legislation. In the hands of a cohesive, skillful minority, the filibuster provides a de facto veto of the entire legislative process. This is important for two reasons. First, when cries of "gridlock" fill the air, the culprit will inevitably be the minority party in the Senate employing the filibuster. This means that when the American people vote in a "unified" government and expect sweeping policy change—as they did in 1992 with President Clinton and a Democratic Congress in 1992, President George W. Bush and a Republican Congress in 2000, and President Barack Obama with large Democratic majorities in 2008—the majority can have its policies frustrated when the minority party in the Senate exercises its "filibuster veto."

Second, in the ultimate legislative irony, when there is bipartisan legislation in the Senate, it is also because of the filibuster. By providing the minority with negotiating leverage, the filibuster forces the majority in the Senate to sit down and negotiate with the minority (something that rarely occurs in the House). This two-sided impact of the filibuster—as both the source of gridlock and bipartisanship—is a nuance missed by those who decry "gridlock" and advocate "bipartisanship." This filibuster paradox contains the corollary that the greater the number of members of the minority in the Senate, and thus the higher the risk of gridlock for a particular bill, the higher the level of bipartisanship required to pass legislation. Senate practitioners have this lesson baked into their bones, but it remains a mystery to their House colleagues and many outside commentators.[23]

Since the 1970s, American presidential candidates have been promising to bring Americans together to enact sweeping bipartisan change.[24] The 2008 campaign for president was only the most recent version of this trend. The major conclusion of this study is that the present mechanics of the American legislative machine —as convincingly demonstrated by the course of the economic stimulus legislation—prevent this from happening. In its present configuration, because of the filibuster in the Senate, the legislative machine can as a general rule produce sweeping PARTISAN change (through a process called reconciliation or, in the alternative, through large partisan majorities that preclude the need for bipartisanship), or incremental, hard-fought BIPARTISAN change: But rapid, sweeping bipartisan change is a rarity. Hopes to the contrary are part of the legislative illusion that grips the country every four years.

As an aside, bipartisanship has become a "Holy Grail" for many commentators. This view has its limits. Bipartisanship is valuable. But there is also a steady stream of mediocre to bad bipartisan legislation. Most earmarks are passed in a bipartisan fashion. Tax bills with heavy special interest input are bipartisan. Bipartisan highway bills are loaded with earmarks and an occasional "bridge to nowhere." In 2008, farmers experienced record levels of income. In a bipartisan manner, Congress passed the most generous program of farm subsidies in history. Subsequently, Congress overrode a presidential veto by overwhelming bipartisan majorities. Bipartisanship is important, but it can also be a convenient excuse for both parties to serve their own interests at the expense of the American taxpayer's.

Although the filibuster is the key to producing both "gridlock" and bipartisan legislation, this can be changed by the members of the Senate at any time. The filibuster is not an immutable condition hard-wired into Senate rules beyond human control. Interestingly, despite past efforts, there have never been enough votes in the Senate to abolish the filibuster.

Ultimately, I believe there are sound reasons for maintaining the filibuster. Among practitioners, there is no dispute that abolishing the filibuster would lead to a substantially more partisan policy process for American democracy. Some of my colleagues from both parties favor such a result. Having survived over the years what I consider to be a barrage of their bad policy ideas, along with viewing with alarm the increasing unity and discipline of the nation's two parties in the twenty-first century, I come down squarely on the side of caution and in favor of keeping the filibuster. But it is precisely the pivotal role played by the filibuster, and the debate surrounding it, that makes it the proper point of focus for any discussion of the future of the American legislative process.

Let me again quote Montaigne, who clearly shared this view:

> It is very doubtful whether there can be such evident profit in changing an accepted law, of whatever sort it be, as there is in disturbing it; inasmuch as a government is like a structure of different parts joined together in such a relation that it is impossible to budge one without the whole body feeling it. The lawmaker of the Thurians ordained that whoever should want either to abolish one of the old laws or to establish a new one should present himself to the people with a rope around his neck; so that if the innovation were not approved by each and every man, he should be promptly strangled.[25]

 CHAPTER 1

The Legislative Machine

The United States has the most intricate legislative machinery on the planet,[1] and the United States Senate has the most permissive rules of any legislative body in the known universe.[2] Dozens of democracies around the globe have no Senate, and occasionally a country will abolish its Senate.

Volumes have been filled with disputes on the intentions of the Founders in setting up the constitutional intricacies of American bicameralism. There is, however, little dispute with the constitutional scholar Edwin Corwin's assessment that the result is "an invitation to struggle."[3] Less noted is that this struggle occurs without any higher authority—a judge, parent, or teacher—to settle a dispute. It is an open-ended and free-form struggle.

Evaluating the performance of this American legislative machine requires familiarity with its mechanics. Much of the recent literature skips this step. Unavoidably, the mechanics matter.

Article I of the Constitution contains the implied requirement that the same language must pass the House of Representatives and Senate before being signed into law by the president. Getting a bill to this stage has generated tomes on legislative procedure for both the House and Senate. Each chamber is filled with rules and precedents, mastered by a cadre of legislative specialists who manage its operations. These rules are also mind-numbing. It is impossible to end a discussion with these procedural purists and have any notion of the strategic "big picture."

The way out of the dilemma of evaluating the key legislative mechanics without undue detail is to use graphic charts—or figures, as they are called here. These do not need to be mastered. Instead, they are designed to provide enough familiarity with the legislative process so that the conclusions based on them make sense.

The Standard Model and Its Flaws

For starters, examine figures 1.1 and 1.2. Figure 1.1 can be called the standard procedure model. This is the model of legislation taught in high school and college. Notice the elegant symmetry as a bill proceeds along its stately course through the House and Senate on its way to the president. Purists call figure 1.1 "regular order."

Figure 1.1. Regular Legislative Order: Standard Procedure Model

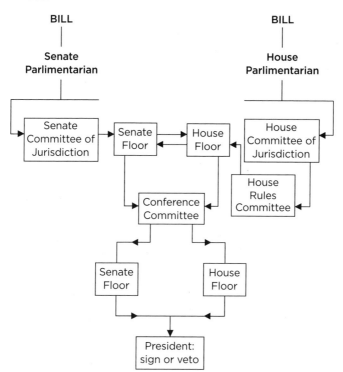

Figure 1.1 has one major flaw. It is rarely followed in practice. Figure 1.2 highlights this shortcoming. Figure 1.2 shows a simplified version of the legislative course run by an obscure bill that Senator Pete Domenici and I worked on in 1978. The bill imposed a small fee on the barge users of federal waterways to recapture a per-

Figure 1.2. A Real-Life Case: Passage in 1978 of the Waterway Trust Fund Legislation

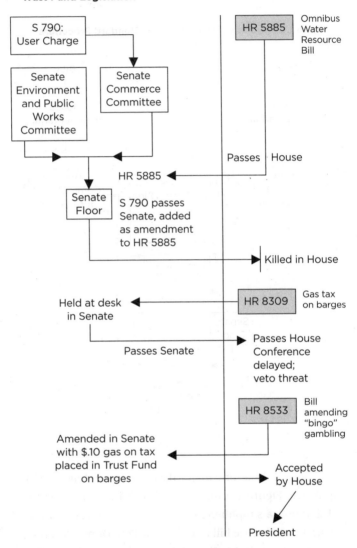

Note: S = Senate resolution; HR = House resolution

centage of the federal costs of building and maintaining these waterways.[4]

Figure 1.2 is a mess. It requires a tortuous explanation, which I will spare you. The purpose of figure 1.2 is to visually highlight the procedural complexity that accompanies even an insignificant bill. The complexity also signals something else: a closely contested, bare-fisted legislative brawl. The barge industry, and its arch-enemy, the railroads, used every weapon at their disposal as they fought each other to the bitter end. It is during this minor legislative spat that I first saw how a veto threat by President Jimmy Carter, threatened filibusters by both parties in the Senate, and a House Rules Committee working at the direction of the speaker of the House, were all interwoven. It is to these three elements—the veto, the filibuster, and the House Rules Committee—that we will soon return below.

Figure 1.2 is also a sample road map to success. Scholars have shown that the more twists and "special procedures" a bill undergoes, the higher its chances of successful enactment. In fact, the prospects of enactment increase from approximately 60 to 80 percent if two or more "special procedures" are used to help pass a bill.[5] Intuitively, this makes sense. The more hotly contested a bill, the more its sponsors and the congressional leadership will need to employ additional legislative procedures to obtain passage. Simple, uncontroversial bills can sail smoothly along. Controversial legislation requires more effort. Flexibility is the key to success. Purists who call for legislation to follow the "regular order" of figure

1.1 either want the legislation to fail or are in denial with respect to the difficulty and extra effort that are required to pass major legislation in the modern Congress.

But figure 1.2 has its shortcomings. Its very complexity obscures the reasons for pivotal strategic and tactical choices. Moreover, there is no assurance that the in-depth study of any individual piece of legislation, no matter how pivotal or complex, will illuminate the underlying structure of the legislative process. My alternative is to substitute the rules of thumb used by legislative practitioners of all political persuasions and weave a crude model out of them. From this effort, certain conclusions about the legislative process naturally flow. These will then allow us to reach a set of crisp conclusions that in turn will allow us to assess the validity of the current legislative orthodoxies.

The Concept of Legislative Terrain

The most basic concept for the legislative practitioner is the notion of legislative terrain: which parties control the House, the Senate, and the presidency. Although obvious, there are subtle consequences that flow from changes in the legislative terrain. Two initial points on legislative terrain are important:

1. The legislative terrain can change every two years. The constitutional scheme provides for elections of the full House and one-third of the Senate every two years, along with presidential elections every fourth year.

2. Changes in the strongholds on the legislative terrain are limited to these options for each year:

Stronghold	Year
House	Democrats or Republicans?
Senate	Democrats or Republicans?
Presidency	Democrats or Republicans?

Putting these two simple points together, it is worth noting the changes in legislative terrain between 1991 and 1995, and between 2003 and 2009, as shown in table 1.1. A cynic might ask, what difference does it make which party holds any of the three strongholds—the House, the Senate, or the presidency? A quick answer from President Bill Clinton's perspective is that without the Republican takeover of the House in the 1994 elections, he would never have been impeached by the House in 1998, even if he was eventually acquitted by the Senate in 1999. From President George W.

Table 1.1. Changes in the Legislative Terrain between 1991 and 1995, and 2003 and 2009 (party in control)

Legislative Stronghold	1991	1993	1995
House	Democrats	Democrats	Republicans
Senate	Democrats	Democrats	Republicans
Presidency	Republicans	Democrats	Democrats

	2003	2005	2009
House	Republicans	Republicans	Democrats
Senate	Republicans	Republicans	Democrats
Presidency	Republicans	Republicans	Democrats

Bush's perspective, after the Democrats retook the House and Senate in 2006, he had to use his veto pen many more times in the following eighteen months than he did the entire six years before. Moreover, in the first six months of Democratic control of the House in 2007, there were 460 oversight hearings,[6] leading to a series of subpoenas aimed at the executive branch. One concerted oversight effort by the House and Senate judiciary committees led to the resignation of Attorney General Alberto Gonzalez in early 2008.

Legislative Strongholds and Arsenals

Having demonstrated the obvious point that shifts in the legislative terrain can have important consequences, it is now time to state the equally obvious point that each of the legislative strongholds—the House, the Senate and the presidency—has unique characteristics. Some of these unique elements are organizational facts—such as the House has 435 members, the Senate has 100 members, but we have only one president at a time.

But legislative practitioners have something different in mind. They are out to define what unique legislative characteristics each stronghold possesses that are not possessed by the others and how these unique characteristics interact with each other.

A learned dissertation would spend the next three chapters deriving, and then justifying, a catalog of the legislative weaponry of each branch. Fortunately, I will show the reader some mercy and simply assert, based on thirty-six years of personal legislative experience, and the concurrence of my fellow practitioners from both sides of the political aisle, that the following simple list provides the essential strongholds and their unique aspects:

Stronghold	*Unique characteristic*
House	Rules Committee
Senate	Filibuster
President	Veto

The "unique characteristic" of each stronghold leads to a simplified view of congressional procedure embodied in the following three questions that can be asked to determine the prospects for enactment of any bill:

- What will the House Rules Committee do?

- Will there be a filibuster in the Senate?

- Will the president veto the bill?

These three questions in turn allow us to reduce the complexities of legislative procedure found in figure 1.1 and 1.2 to the bare-bones triangle shown in figure 1.3.[7]

Figure 1.3. A Triangle That Simplifies the Complexities of Legislative Procedure

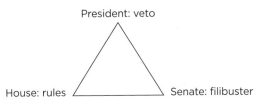

President: veto

House: rules   Senate: filibuster

This simplified procedural scheme has another virtue: It identifies the three critical points of leverage that effectively determine the nature of the legislative process in modern America. It is now time to discuss the three points of leverage separately.

 CHAPTER 2

Moving Parts: The Veto and the House Rules Committee

The Veto

Because it is based on the Constitution (Article I, Section 7), the president's veto is a good place to start before we take more in-depth looks at the legislative nuances of the House of Representatives and Senate. The important thing about the veto is that it requires majorities of two-thirds of the House and Senate to be overridden. If a president can muster the support of one-third plus one of the members of either chamber, he can wipe out the legislative effort of large congressional majorities. Thus a president and 34 senators (one-third of the Senate plus one) can negate the efforts of 501 other members of Congress (66 senators and 435 House members).

Despite its powerful legislative impact, it is worth stressing that the veto is a defensive weapon.[1] It can kill, but not initiate, legislation. However, because of its extreme legislative consequences and the difficulty in overriding it, the veto is a strong bargaining chip with Congress, and it will often lead Congress to accommodate presidential concerns. But the threat cannot be an idle one. In the late 1970s, when President Jimmy Carter first threatened, then blinked, on a veto of congressional water projects, his administration never recovered its credibility with Congress.

House Rules: Origins

It is now time to take a closer look at figure 1.1 in chapter 1 above. Although originally described as a textbook example of the symmetrical passage of a bill through the House and Senate, a closer look shows one crucial anomaly: In the House, there is a detour for a bill between full committee and the House floor that goes through the House Rules Committee.

For years, I have been telling my students at William and Mary that the House Rules Committee is democracy's equivalent of Stalin's politburo. I had occasional pangs of guilt over the analogy until I read a *New York Times* analysis of the Rules Committee noting that it "resembles the Central Committee of the Communist Party in the old Soviet Union."[2]

One of the constants of Washington is the howls of pain of the minority party in the House as it rails against the tyranny of the House majority. Republicans spent forty years before 1994 calling for "open rules" on the

House floor so that bills could be fairly debated and amended. During the Republican ascendancy after 1994, the same cry could be heard from Democrats. In fact, it was their howls of pain that triggered some of the negative commentary in *The Broken Branch, Fight Club Politics*, and *The Second Civil War*. The consensus view of these commentators was that while Democrat abuses "flowed from the insularity and arrogance of power that came from nearly forty years of unbridled majority,"[3] the Republican-controlled Congress was "worse." With the election of a Democratic House in 2006, there was the ritualistic paying of homage to "civility," "collegiality," and a general commitment to "open, full, and fair debate" by the new Democratic House leadership.[4] But as the press and some informed commentators have noted, there has been no substantive change in the tradition of "hardball" in legislating in the House under the New Democratic leadership.[5] At this juncture, it would be easy to slip into a practiced cynical commentary on politics or the legislative process. It is also usually considered de rigueur at this point to offer some solutions to either foster civility or minority rights in the House. Neither cynicism nor solutions are necessary, however.

The minority in the House of Representatives has been boiling over at its plight for almost 120 years. This condition has persisted regardless of party or personalities. Obviously, there are structural or fundamental human elements at play that go beyond the moment or any recent cataloging of the sins of one's opponents. The House Rules Committee is a creature of the leadership of the majority of the House. Its ostensible purpose is to set the rules for debate for the floor of the House. Its real purpose is to ensure victory for the majority party.

Establishing and perfecting this majoritarian regime has taken the House well over a century. It began with Speaker Tom Reed in 1890, who instituted a set of reforms expanding the role of the Rules Committee and curtailing minority rights. This earned him the title of "Czar Reed." Before Rules Committee meetings, he would invite the minority in and inform them: "Here is an outrage McKinley, Cannon, and myself are about to perpetrate. You will have time to prepare your screams and usual denunciations."[6]

Reed's majoritarian machine underwent further refinement in the early twentieth century when power switched between the parties three times, and each time minority rights were circumscribed.[7] But final refinements had to wait until the 1970s and 1980s. Beginning in the 1960s, Northern liberals launched an internecine struggle with their Southern Democratic colleagues for control of the House. At the outset, by relying on their seniority, the South had control of the House through an interlocking directorate of committee chairmen, including the chairmanship of the Rules Committee. Northern liberals in a series of struggles jettisoned the seniority system and brought the powerful Southern chairmen to heel. During the course of the ten Congresses from 1965 to 1985, minority rights were curtailed in eight.[8] Twice, in 1971 and 1975, liberal Democrats reached out with concessions to gain Republican votes in the liberals' struggle with their Southern colleagues. Each time, after power was consolidated, the concessions to minority rights were repealed.[9]

The liberals were after more than procedural advantage. They had a purpose. They wanted to pass a liberal agenda, starting with major civil rights legislation. Thus, the liberals "aggressively pursued procedural solutions to secure preferred policy outcomes."[10] They had an agenda, and they planned on winning.

The House Rules Committee in Action

This is the machine that the Republicans inherited with their victory in 1994, and that was recaptured by the Democrats in 2006. It consists an arsenal of techniques perfected over a hundred years to ensure victory for the majority party. The most powerful of these techniques is the "closed rule," which consists of denying any floor amendments. For example, in 2007 during the debate on a children's health bill (known as SCHIP), the Rules Committee received forty-three requests to amend the bill on the House floor. None were granted. In cases where amendments are needed, the Rules Committee can allow for a "structured rule," which means that only carefully tailored amendments guaranteed to succeed are allowed. In addition, over the years, both parties have perfected what are known as self-executing rules. This legislative creation provides that when the rule for a bill is adopted, a set of attached amendments are automatically adopted, sparing the majority the need to vote on any of them. The chance for mischief with these self-executing rules is infinite. The existence of this species of self-executing rules only reinforces the central premise that in the House the majority will prevail by virtually any means available.[11]

My favorite example of the arbitrary power of the House Rules Committee is old and minor, but it is singed into my memory because I was a victim. In 1991, I was at the Department of Justice and assisting the George H. W. Bush administration in pushing for an amendment to limit death sentence appeals, called habeas corpus reform. The amendment had two parts. The first limited the rights of appeal of those on death row. The second provided funds to state prosecutors to pursue death penalty cases through the expensive appeals process. The prosecutors, particularly from the Southern states, were lobbying hard for the amendment. The majority Democratic leaders of the House realized that they could not jettison the amendment, but that if they allowed a vote they risked losing many Southern Democrats on a law-and-order issue. When Representative Henry Hyde (Ill.), a senior Republican, and the sponsor of the amendment, appeared before the Rules Committee, he was given startling news. The Rules Committee ordered that his amendment be split and offered as two amendments. Hyde rightfully objected, making the obvious point that he should be allowed to write his amendment the way he wanted, an appeal that fell on deaf ears. By splitting the amendment, the Rules Committee allowed Southern Democrats to make their local prosecutors happy by voting for money for them, thus freeing them to reject limitations on death penalty appeals. This legislative gambit delayed reform for five years before a Republican Congress finally passed comprehensive habeas corpus reform in 1996.

The options available to a House minority in response to the manipulations of the Rules Committee are limited. The principal one is a "motion to recommit" the bill.[12] This means that the bill can be withdrawn from consideration on the House floor and returned to the committee of jurisdiction. Such a rule can also provide the bill is to be reported back "forthwith." This important nuance means that the minority is guaranteed a final amendment, which can instantly change the bill if adopted. Motions to recommit are rarely successful. Regardless of the merits, such motions are treated as direct attacks on the majority leadership. The majority leadership will often punish majority members who stray on such test votes.

The Culture of Winner Take All

In a winner-take-all political contest, it is not unusual for the loser to feel aggrieved. During most of the forty years of unbroken control of the House by the Democrats, the Republicans were not a serious competitor for control. Accordingly, the parties settled into a comfortable arrangement, characterized by Ronald Brownstein as "the widespread belief among Democrats that they represented the country's natural majority party."[13]

With shifts in power in 1994 and 2006, both sides have begun fashioning the kind of mythology around victory and loss that characterizes politics in the Balkans.

These "Balkan War" tales from the House of Representatives, now embedded in the media consensus on American politics, offer an opening to discuss the role of human failings in politics. A substantial body of experimental data shows that when injured parties retaliate, they invariably inflict additional harm on their victim beyond what they suffered, even if they believe they are carefully responding in equal measure.

An experiment demonstrates this phenomenon. Two adults face each other, each with the ability to depress a small metal bar on the finger of the other. Both are given the same instruction: Match exactly the force received from the other. As the two begin to alternately press the bar on each other, the force escalates dramatically. At the end, each participant tells the instructor that the other adult had been told to press "twice as hard." In nine exchanges, the force escalated twentyfold. In neuroscience, this is known as the "two eyes for an eye" doctrine.[14] This small scientific insight shows why it is extremely difficult—in my view, impossible—to sort out the major culprit in escalating political feuds. When commentators designate either Democrats or Republicans as "worse" than the other in a political struggle, they are probably falling victim to this flaw in human nature.[15]

Most of the critiques of the modern legislative process note the lack of "comity" between members and then cite as evidence some recent harsh exchange between House members. An oft-cited one has Republican representative Scott McGinnis (Colo.) telling Democratic representative Fortney "Pete" Stark (Calif.) to "shut up" during a legislative markup and Stark responding, "You think you are big enough you little wimp? Come on, come on over and make me, I dare you, you little fruit-cake."[16]

Even the harshest critics, admit, however, that this exchange is mild in relation to the fatal duels, murders (two I am aware of), brawls, punches, use of fire tongs, and brandishing of pistols that characterized the nineteenth-century House and Senate.[17] In fact, the first Congress gave its sergeant at arms a mace, a medieval weapon, for a purpose. Based on experience, they knew that legislatures could erupt into brawls. Today, the mace is a symbolic accoutrement, but in the nineteenth century it was occasionally wielded.

My favorite episode occurred during the lead-up to the Civil War. In a late-night session in 1858, Representative Lawrence Keitt of South Carolina called his Pennsylvania colleague, Representative Galusha Grow, "a black Republican puppy," to which Grow responded "No Negro-driver shall crack the whip over me." Fifty men charged each other, punching, kicking, and ignoring all cries for "order." Reporters got into the spirit of the event by cracking "smutty jokes" and firing "spit-balls" at each other. The sergeant at arms brandished his mace. The brawl turned to farce when one member reached for the hair of an opponent and pulled off his wig. "I've scalped him," he cried, and the brawlers dissolved into laughter.[18]

This little episode has several lessons. The first is that today's Congress is tame compared with its nineteenth-century predecessors. I am unaware of a solid punch being delivered and connecting in the House or Senate for at least twenty years. We look to informed commentators and academics for perspective, not hype.

In addition, the commentary on the modern Congress ignores the emotional intensity of the legislative process. A very combustible package of drives and emotions gives the legislative process its energy. Some discussions rightfully discuss ambition and ego, one commentator creatively labeling Washington a "domed ego-farm."[19] But there are other emotions that do not draw the same attention. One is a package of "moral emotions" with which humans may be born. The importance of this for the legislative process is that issues of policy become issues of "right and wrong." If you propose universal health care as a "moral right," a common position today, your opponents are not simply disagreeing—they are "wrong." This triggers the emotion of righteous anger and the demand for punishment—a form of authorized aggression—against those who oppose you.[20] The emotional volatility brought on by these moral elements is ratcheted up by competitive considerations. Members of Congress must compete to get elected, and they must repeatedly win elections to keep their seats. Parties compete with each other to achieve and maintain dominance in the House, Senate, and presidency. The goal of competition is triumph. We need to be candid enough about ourselves to admit that in a competitive situation, "like a lawyer, the human brain wants victory, not truth."[21]

The ease with which humans can be divided into opposing groups is well documented. The cognitive scientist Stephen Pinker calls this "instant ethnocentrism." In one experiment, middle-class American boys at a summer camp were randomly divided into two groups that competed in sports and skits. Within days, the boys were attacking each other with sticks, bats, and rocks. The experimenters had to intervene for the sake of the safety of the boys.[22] The emotional intensity of the legislative process is often dismissed as a failing of individual members or particular parties. This ignores the deep human instincts that are triggered by the competitive forum of the legislative process. The intensity is not a result of moral failings. It is simply a product of humans competing, or what scientists call the "in-group/out-group bias," which is both "universal and ineradicable."[23]

There is a great deal at stake in this competition. Winners not only capture the rulemaking machinery of a society but also determine the substance of these rules. In fact, all around the globe and all throughout history, the power over others that comes with victory in political competitions has led parties to pick up guns to prevail. In comparison with the bloody ethnic, religious, and political strife that dominates the front pages of our newspapers today, calling someone a "fruitcake" is hardly worth noting.

This seeming digression actually has a point. The science of human nature has established that comity and cooperation require enforcement of the rules. Cooperative situations without enforcement degenerate into situations where people go their own way, or, in game theory terms, "defect." In fact, over time, when given the chance, people will abandon situations where there is no enforcement of the rules of cooperation and move to situations where the rules are enforced.[24]

Interestingly, the need for comity as a precondition for cooperation has been overstated. Comity makes for a more cordial working relationship, but it is a second-order virtue in the legislative process. Proof that cooperation can exist without comity comes from that most extreme of human activities: war. In his classic study of cooperation, Robert Axelrod tells the astonishing tale of how German, British, and French soldiers facing each other in the trenches of World War I spontaneously evolved their own cooperative "live and let live" strategy. Artillerymen, machine gunners, and riflemen on both sides would intentionally miss their targets. But a retaliatory enforcement capability was continuously demonstrated. The artillery would pick out a difficult target and demolish it, or snipers—particularly the feared German snipers—would fire repeatedly at a spot on a wall and create a hole to demonstrate their prowess. In case of a violation, the offended party would retaliate at a ratio of two or three to one until order was again established. The system eventually collapsed as the military leadership of both sides recognized the situation and began to rotate troops more quickly in and out of the trenches. In addition, the leadership began to order raids against enemy lines that forced the soldiers in the trenches to defend themselves.[25]

The relevance of this for our purposes is that as long as the House of Representatives organizes itself as a disciplined, centralized machine exclusively for victory for the majority party, there will not be lasting comity or cooperation in the House if the two political parties are competitive. Thus, the House floor has many elements of a winner-take-all situation.[26] Occasionally, there will be interludes where the parties will cooperate out of necessity. This will occur in cases where the minority has political leverage. There will also be moments where the two parties talk of cooperation and respecting minority interests, but this will collapse under the stress of close votes and the competition for control. Without consistent negotiating leverage, cooperation and comity are always at risk on the House floor.

The minutes of a conference at Princeton University in December 2004 contained the following insightful comment by Representative Tom Cole (R-Okla.), during an exchange with former representative Philip Sharp (D-Ind.). "But" Cole continued, "I would argue that in so far as the Democrats ever negotiated with Republicans it was because they had to. . . . You don't include the other side if you can get there with your own," he said. Phillip Sharp made this same point in a different way: "We don't have bipartisanship, and we never had it, for bipartisanship's sake," he said. "The reason you have bipartisanship is because it's necessary for political reasons. Bipartisanship really happens when there's a reason for it to happen."[27]

If the American legislative process were unicameral, the lack of minority rights on the House floor, along with the inevitable dustups between the members, would be of concern. But the Constitution provides for a Senate. Though the House is designed for offense, the Senate has perfected the art of playing legislative defense. Assessing the performance of the American legislative system requires looking separately at the Senate, and then judging how the Senate, the House, and the president interact as a single system.

 CHAPTER 3

The Filibuster and the Minority Tool Kit

Origins of the Filibuster

Colonial Pennsylvania, where Benjamin Franklin practiced his politics, had a unicameral legislature. Franklin thought that bicameralism was "like putting a horse before a cart and the other behind it and whipping them both. If the horses are of equal strength, the wheels of the cart, like the wheels of government, will stand still; and if the horses are strong enough, the cart will be torn to pieces."[1] Franklin's view of bicameralism did not prevail at the Constitutional Convention, but he accurately forecast the difficulties posed by adding a Senate to the legislative process.

If the House of Representatives fashioned itself into a majoritarian body designed to take the offensive in the legislative process, the Senate has perfected the art of legislative defense. But in contrast to the House's conscious, goal-oriented efforts, the Senate's perfection of its defensive skills has been the result of an unintended legislative mutation: the filibuster.[2] When commentators criticize government "gridlock," it is the filibuster they are attacking. With a threshold of 41 senators, the filibuster allows the minority in the Senate to gain virtual control of the entire Senate. This control can become so pervasive as to constitute a de facto legislative veto. Under skillful direction, a minority in the Senate can dominate the legislative process for the entire federal establishment.

In 1806, when the Senate was revising and cleaning up "a messy rulebook," it dropped the rule known as "calling the previous question."[3] In 1806, the senators saw no need for the rule; and in fact, it had been used in some cases to interrupt fruitful debate.[4] The House kept the "previous question rule," and later in the nineteenth century reengineered it to use it to end debate and force a vote on an issue. The Senate, without such a rule, had no such parliamentary weapon at hand. From this small difference in institutional history, the two bodies were launched on separate evolutionary trajectories.

The filibuster mutation lay relatively dormant in the Senate until 1841, when opponents of Henry Clay's bank bill organized to exploit the lack of a previous question rule to extend debate. After Clay threatened to change the rules on them,[5] they folded. After that, the "filibuster" mutation spread until it dominated the Senate by the late 1890s. Several quotations from the nine-

teenth-century Senate will spare an elaborate set of ex-
planations. For starters, here is Senator Thomas Hart
Benton (D-Mo.) on the origins of the filibuster in 1841:

> He [Mr. Clay] was impatient to pass his bills, annoyed at
> the resistance they met, and dreadfully harassed by the
> species of warfare to which they were subjected; and for
> which he had no turn. The democratic senators acted
> upon a system, and with a thorough organization, and
> a perfect understanding. Being a minority, and able to
> do nothing, they became assailants, and attacked inces-
> santly; not by formal orations against the whole body of
> a measure, but by sudden, short and pungent speeches,
> directed against the vulnerable parts; and pointed by
> proffered amendments. Amendments were continuously
> offered—a great number being prepared every night,
> and placed in suitable hands the next day.[6]

In 1852, Senator Willie Magnum (Whig-N.C.) mourned
the new lack of restraint in the Senate:

> In the older and better times of the Senate, it was sup-
> posed that the representatives of sovereign States, from
> a proper sense of what was due to themselves, as well as
> what was due this body, . . . would restrain themselves
> from the excessive use of irrelevant talking. Modern ex-
> perience, however, has shown that this feeling, as a re-
> straint, is utterly insufficient for the purpose of correct-
> ing this abuse.[7]

Finally, here is Senator John Sherman (R-Ohio) in
1865:

> At this hour we are within five days of the close of the
> session, and we have not acted upon a single appropri-
> ation bill finally. . . . Under the circumstance I cannot,

with my sense of public duty, allow the Louisiana question to consume more time.[8]

These quotations establish that by the mid–nineteenth century, the basic strategic elements of the filibuster were in place. Senator Benton's characterization
of a "system" of obstruction, not just speeches, against
Clay's program highlights the fact that there is a "Minority Tool Kit" for obstruction in the Senate. Senator
Magnum's observation has two important elements.
First, when he notes a lack of "restraint," he is signaling
that like any successful tactic, the filibuster was already
spreading rapidly throughout the Senate's culture by the
1850s. Second, his reference to "older and better times"
is a staple of even modern commentary on the filibuster.
Invariably, this commentary spreads pixie dust on a previous era, declaring it "older and better." And when Senator Sherman speaks of the "Louisiana question," this is
not a small matter. This was a filibuster by Lincoln's own
Republicans against his effort to have Louisiana read-
mitted to the Union at the end of the Civil War. The use
of the filibuster at the end of sessions to kill legislation
was to increase, which highlights how the filibuster is
used to run out the clock at the end of a congressional
session.

A reader should ask at this juncture what is the difference between the emotional tenor of these quotations and any recent lamentations on the Senate that
they have heard from a learned commentator, former
senator, or even sitting senator? The answer: None.

Senator Magnum's fear of lack of "restraint" contin-ued until, by the end of the nineteenth century, the Sen-ate became "unmanageable."[9] For those who compare today's lack of "comity" with past golden eras, the fol-lowing characterization of the late-nineteenth-century filibuster by Franklin Burdette, one of the early students of the filibuster, should dampen this line of criticism:

> If dilatory tactics upon the Senate floor, increasing in turbulence and boldness for more than fifty years, had largely been fruitless expenditures of energy in a parlia-mentary sense, the closing decades of the nineteenth century gave way to another story. . . . Ruthlessness and obstruction began to be bounded by only the ingenuity of its designers. If courtesy required restraint, it was for-gotten; if dignity demanded moderation, it was sacri-ficed to political or sectional advantage.[10]

Most successful strategies have the seeds of their own demise embedded within them. The nineteenth-cen-tury filibusters could not be stopped. Eventually, Sena-tor Magnum's observation that its proponents lacked "restraint" proved prescient. In 1917, with German sub-marines sinking American merchant vessels, President Woodrow Wilson proposed to arm them. Senator Robert La Follette and others, wishing to keep America out of World War I, launched a filibuster. The Senate then ad-journed without acting. President Wilson popped his cork against this "little group of willful men." The Amer-ican people followed suit. Wilson armed the vessels by executive order and then called the Senate back into ses-sion to change the rules to limit filibusters. The Senate, humiliated and seeing that the game was over, quickly responded by voting 76–3 to allow two-thirds of the Senate to cut off debate. Thus was born Rule 22 in the Senate, also known as cloture. In some dense parliamentary maneuvering, the two-thirds requirement to invoke cloture was changed to three-fifths, or 60 votes, in 1975. When commentators talk of a "supermajority" or a "60-vote Senate," they are referring to today's Rule 22, the basic outlines of which were established in 1975.[11]

The Mechanics of the Filibuster

Because of the central role played by the filibuster in the American legislative process, it is essential to delve deeper into its mechanics. At the outset, one caveat is in order. Above, the filibuster was labeled a "de facto legislative veto." There is one major exception to this generalization. It is called reconciliation, and it operates under a statutory time limit of twenty hours for debate, thus precluding any filibusters. In the next chapter, we will note specific circumstances relating to the federal budget and taxes where the reconciliation process allows for a majority vote (51 votes) in the Senate to pass a bill. But outside the confines of reconciliation, a successful filibuster generally acts as an absolute bar to the passage of legislation, just like a successful presidential veto.

Senate floor procedure is based on a model of unlimited debate. Senators get to talk until they are ready to vote. There are two ways to limit debate. First, all senators can agree on how to structure the debate (i.e., two hours for amendments) and when to vote on final passage (i.e., Tuesday at 2:00 PM). Such agreements are called "unanimous consent agreements" or "time agreements." Pursuing such agreements has the obvious shortcoming that one senator can scuttle the agreement by withholding consent.

The second method for ending debate is the cloture process found in Rule 22. If one or a group of senators refuses to end debate, they have begun a filibuster. Rule 22 lays out a precise procedure for ending filibusters, with these principal steps:

1. Sixteen or more senators file a cloture motion to end debate.

2. After filing a cloture motion, the Senate must wait an intervening calendar day, plus one hour after convening, before a vote is taken in support of the motion.

3. If the motion receives 60 votes and passes, there are thirty hours of debate left, after which a vote on final passage occurs. (Gaining cloture by a 60-vote majority has other benefits. One is that nongermane amendments, discussed below, are out of order after cloture is invoked.)

There are a variety of elegant nuances to this three-step process that will be mercifully ignored. Two, however, are worth discussing. First, to partially repeat ourselves, if the majority does not get 60 votes, and the cloture petition fails, the bill is dead. Finito.[12] There is a second, less recognized consequence of the filibuster: control of the legislative calendar. Table 3.1 shows the timing implications of a hypothetical filibuster.

Notice how five working days, or a full legislative week, are consumed with defeating a filibuster and passing the underlying legislation through the Senate. Obviously, the process is sometimes expedited, but any time gained on an individual bill can be negated by the Senate minority triggering concurrent and sequential filibusters. Even a successful cloture motion that gets 60 votes and defeats a filibuster has elements of a Pyrrhic victory because of the steep price of losing substantial time during a legislative session. Thus, a minority in the Senate that uses the filibuster gains an advantage in both victory and defeat. A win kills undesirable legislation. A loss reduces the time available to the majority to consider other parts of its agenda.

In the fall of 1994, then Republican minority leader Senator Robert Dole (R-Kans.) orchestrated five simultaneous filibusters whose overlapping impact gave him procedural and thus substantive control of the Senate.

Table 3.1. A Hypothetical Filibuster

Monday	Tuesday	Wednesday	Thursday	Friday
Begin filibuster	Cloture motion, noon	1 day	10:00 AM: cloture vote; if passes, 30 hours (runs overnight)	4:30 PM: final passage

Only those bills that he agreed to passed the Senate. President Bill Clinton and the Democratic majorities in the House and Senate watched helplessly. In 1996, after the Republicans had regained the majority in the Senate in 1994, Senator Dole ran for president. It was time for payback. The Senate Democratic minority leader, Tom Daschle (S.D.) used the same script to seize control of the Senate before the 1996 presidential and congressional elections.

Completing the Minority Tool Kit:
Germaneness and Holds

With the basic procedural triangle of the veto, the House Rules Committee, and the Senate filibuster in place, it is apparent that the defense has a marked advantage in the legislative process. Two of the three—the veto and filibuster—require supermajorities for passage, increasing the difficulty of enacting legislation.

In addition to the filibuster, the Senate has two other tactics—nongermane amendments, and holds—that, when integrated with the filibuster, form the Minority Tool Kit. The filibuster remains the centerpiece of the Minority Tool Kit, but the other two work in concert with the filibuster and augment its leverage. For discussion purposes, let us start with nongermane amendments.

In the House of Representatives, an amendment has to relate to the subject matter of the bill, a sensible and logical requirement. An amendment to an immigration bill must relate to immigration; an amendment to a farm bill must relate to agriculture. In the Senate, there is no such requirement. An amendment on nuclear weapons can be attached to an education bill.[13]

The tactical, even strategic, advantages this procedural nuance provides to the minority are significant. Nongermane amendments provide a mechanism for the minority to simply change the subject. It allows for a direct challenge by the minority to the ability of the majority in the Senate to set the legislative agenda and determine the timing of its consideration.

For example, let us return to Senator Dole's 1996 presidential run. In April 1996, Senator Dole, after clinching the Republican nomination for president, announced during a Florida vacation that he would return to the Senate and use it as a platform for wresting the presidency from Bill Clinton. The first bill he brought onto the Senate floor upon his return was an immigration measure. The first amendment, offered by Senator Ted Kennedy (D-Mass.), was to raise the minimum wage. The resulting procedural snafu tied the Senate floor in knots for three weeks, left Senator Dole's hope of using the Senate floor as a platform for his presidential bid in shambles, and subsequently forced his resignation as Senate majority leader to save his campaign further embarrassment.

Often, the filibuster and nongermane amendments are used in combination by the minority. If the majority obtains the 60 votes it needs to end debate and invokes cloture, a germaneness requirement comes automatically with the successful cloture vote. There are, however, cases where the minority does not want to defeat legislation but simply wants to add nongermane amendments to it.[14] To do this, the minority must first defeat cloture, and then it can pursue its strategy of offering nongermane amendments to the bill.[15]

This combination of filibusters and nongermane amendments is a flexible, powerful one-two punch for the minority. Filibusters can be used to either kill legislation or set up a series of nongermane amendments on subjects the majority wants to avoid. The crucial calculation by the minority is how important is the legislation to the majority, and thus how much grief the majority is willing to endure to pass the bill. In 2003, Senator Richard Lugar (R-Ind.) brought his Department of State reauthorization bill to the Senate floor. The Democratic minority responded with a wave of nongermane amendments. The majority decided that the bill was not worth the struggle, and simply pulled it off the Senate floor.

In contrast, in 2004, the Republican majority was under pressure to pass a corporate tax bill called FSC/ETI.[16] The initials are irrelevant, but the situation was urgent. A U.S. international tax code provision had been ruled illegal, and European countries were imposing penalties on U.S. goods entering Europe. The minority fought off several cloture motions, thereby enabling it to force a vote on a nongermane amendment to overturn overtime regulations that were objectionable to labor unions and the Democratic minority. To add salt to the wound, once the minority got a commitment for an up-or-down vote on this amendment, the minority picked up enough votes from moderate Republicans to win. With this victory in hand, the bill then passed the Senate.

A different calculation in 2004 was made on civil justice reform legislation. The majority had enough votes to gain cloture, but the moderate Democrats who supported cloture imposed a condition on their support that the majority must allow votes on a series of nongermane amendments, including raising the federal minimum wage and addressing climate change. Again, as with the State Department authorization bill for the previous year, the majority decided passing this bill was not worth the price.

The final moving part in the Minority Tool Kit is "the hold." In theory, this is just a request by a senator to be notified when legislation is going to be considered on the Senate floor. This is a perfectly legitimate requirement. Often, at the end of a session, or before a recess, dozens of bills will fly through the Senate in hours. And occasionally, a little chicanery is involved.

But the request for notification implies more. Holds have evolved into an initial statement by an individual senator or group of senators that they intend to either filibuster or negotiate changes to the subject bill (or in some cases, some other bill of interest, using the subject bill as a "hostage").[17] From the initial negotiations on the holds on a particular bill, the majority and minority can determine their relative positions. From the majority's viewpoint, the hold discussions establish whether negotiated changes will be enough to allow the bill to pass, or whether a full-fledged cloture fight, with an array of nongermane amendments, is on the horizon. In turn, the minority can gauge how much pain the majority is willing to suffer through negotiations or how much time the majority is willing to spend on the Senate floor to pass a particular bill. Because these negotiations are a continuous, daily occurrence, both sides are able to quickly size up the determination of the other. There are few surprises in this process.

With this discussion of nongermane amendments and holds under our belts, we can chart the complete Minority Tool Kit. The filibuster and nongermane amendments represent the visible parts of the tool kit on the Senate floor. Because these are matters of public record, and easily quantified, they receive the most attention. But they are in fact only part of the tool kit. Beneath the surface, the holds have an equal effect. Also, as noted above, filibusters, whether successful or not, chew up the valuable commodity of the time available for the Senate to address the range of issues before it. Barbara Sinclair has called the filibuster the "tip of the iceberg" of the delaying tactics available to the minority. Taking this analogy more literally than she probably intended, we can provide figure 3.1, which shows the "iceberg" created by the Minority Tool Kit in the Senate.[18]

Concluding Note

As Senator Benton observed about the first filibuster in 1841, the minority uses a "system" to obstruct in the Senate. For 168 years, the "system" has continued to evolve and be refined by minorities of both parties. To-

Figure 3.1. The Senate Iceberg

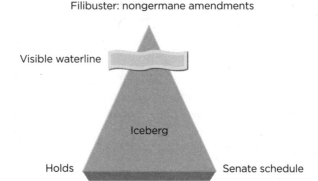

day, if supported by 41 votes, it is impenetrable, an absolute bar, a de facto legislative veto. This leads to the conclusion that the key variable in the American legislative process is whether the majority in the Senate can muster 60 votes.

This conclusion contains an unappreciated truism. For the last thirty years, no party has held more than 60 seats in the United States Senate. This means that legislation *must be* bipartisan to pass the Senate. Though commentators and academics have been decrying "polarization and hyperpartisanship," the actual mechanics of the legislative process in the Senate force bipartisanship. Because of the Senate's role in the legislative process, as a matter of legislative logic, most legislation must be bipartisan to reach the president. The only major exception to this is a process referred to before as reconciliation, to which we will now turn.

 CHAPTER 4

Legislative Dialectics and the Birth of Reconciliation

The Birth of Reconciliation

The Senate is the breeding ground for legislative mutations. The filibuster, the product of a rules change that had largely unanticipated consequences, has become the most powerful defensive weapon in the legislative arsenal. One of the most powerful offensive weapons, reconciliation, is also the result of a Senate mutation.

In 1981, a new Republican president, Ronald Reagan, and a new Senate majority leader, Howard Baker (R-Tenn.), were faced with a dilemma. During his campaign, President Reagan had promised domestic spending cuts. The effort to translate this part of his agenda from campaign rhetoric into legislative reality faced two challenges. The first was a Democratic majority in the House of Representatives. Surprisingly, presidential advisers believed that a large bloc of southern Democrats would give President Reagan a working majority in the House.

Of more concern was the second roadblock: the certainty of a Democratic filibuster in the Senate. With a 53–47 majority, the nominally Republican Senate was at the mercy of the Democrats' 40-plus-vote minority. This dilemma led to a series of meetings in Howard Baker's basement over several weeks with the troika of David Stockman, director of the Office of Management and Budget, Baker, the Senate majority leader, and Senator Pete Domenici (R-N.M.), chairman of the Senate Budget Committee.

The result of these deliberations was to bet the Reagan presidency on a provision of the Democratic-passed 1974 Budget Act that was virtually untested.[1] The irony of using legislation that had been fashioned by the Democrats to help in their budget struggle with President Richard Nixon to ram through President Reagan's budget cuts over fierce Democratic resistance was obvious to all sides.

The chosen vehicle for this offensive thrust was Section 310 of the Budget Act, titled "Reconciliation." Now, with the passage of twenty-seven years since the Reagan gamble, reconciliation has become a familiar term of art in the legislative process.[2] Less recognized is the minor role originally conceived for it. Reconciliation was originally designed to be used as a year-end mop-up operation for the budgetary process. At the end of the fiscal year, if Congress during the course of the year had missed its budgetary targets, reconciliation was available to make up the difference. Because reconciliation was designed to occur at the end of the budgetary process, and thus toward the end of the legislative year, it was provided procedural protection against minority delaying tactics, such as filibusters and nongermane amendments. There was to be a limit of twenty hours of debate. Fifty-one votes would be enough to ensure passage.

Reagan, copying Marx's treatment of Hegel, stood reconciliation on its head. (Regrettably, this is what passes for legislative wit.) Instead of using reconciliation for the modest purpose of closing the books at the end of the budgetary year, Reagan moved reconciliation to the start of the legislative year. He then jammed his spending cuts into the reconciliation process. Using the special procedural protections afforded by reconciliation, Senators Baker and Domenici then beat back a series of Democratic challenges with a 51-vote majority. Against the 60-vote threshold needed to end a filibuster, the Reagan budget cuts would have been legislative dead meat.

The Reconciliation Dialectic: Expansion and the Byrd Amendment

The value of reconciliation for those wishing to take the legislative offensive became readily apparent, particularly in the Senate. The leaders of the majority party in the Senate realized that they had stumbled on a procedural weapon that matched the House Rules Committee. The filibuster and other nongermane defensive measures were circumvented. The Senate had become a majoritarian forum like the House—51 votes meant victory.

With such a powerful legislative mutation at their disposal, Senate majorities made regular use of reconciliation. Between 1981 and 1990, reconciliation legislation became a standard feature of the budgetary process.[3]

Legislative practitioners quickly began to expand the role of reconciliation beyond its original focus on taxes and entitlement spending. In legislative jargon, reconciliation is an ideal "vehicle." Because of its procedural safeguards, any member of Congress, or an interest group with a legislative proposal, would have the prospects for successful enactment substantially enhanced if it became part of a reconciliation bill. It was not long before legislative proposals with no relationship to the Budget Act began to appear in reconciliation. Legislation on such diverse matters as trade policy, nuclear waste disposal, and the "fairness doctrine" for broadcasters became law under the procedural protections of reconciliation.

A counterattack was not long in coming. Senator Robert Byrd (D-W.Va.), the most senior and one of the most skilled members of the Senate, decried the Pandora's box that had been opened by the "abuse" of the reconciliation process. In 1985, Senator Byrd wrote an amendment to the Budget Act known as the "Byrd Rule." Although complex, the amendment's purpose is a straightforward attack on "extraneous provisions" to reconciliation. It declares a provision to be "extraneous" if it has no budgetary impact or if its budgetary effects are "merely incidental" to its core purposes. If the Senate parliamentarian rules a matter "extraneous" under the Byrd rule, it takes 60 votes to overturn such a ruling.

Over time, the Byrd Rule has proven a powerful check on the scope of reconciliation. In 1993, more than 150 provisions passed by a Democratic House were dropped in the Senate because of Byrd Rule objections. In 1995, it was Senate Republicans' turn to suffer as 170 provisions of their reconciliation bill, by my unofficial count, were dropped in the Senate. It is still common for House majorities to complain bitterly about its limiting effect when their bills reach the Senate. It may also have led to a decline in the use of reconciliation itself. In the twenty-three years since 1985, reconciliation has been used fourteen times, three of which were vetoed by President Bill Clinton.

Concluding Note

This description of the reconciliation process and the Byrd Rule brings us to the end of our discussion of the major moving parts in the legislative machine. This also provides an excuse for an updated figure and table. Figure 4.1 updates our triangle given in figure 1.3—which simplified the complexities of legislative procedure—by showing the major moving parts, adding reconciliation and the Byrd Rule. The upper triangle still gives the major points of leverage in the legislative process, and the

Figure 4.1. Updated Triangles Showing the Major Moving Parts in the Legislative Machine

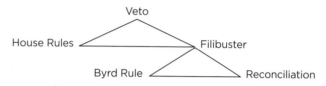

lower triangle fleshes out the points of leverage in the Senate. The lower, Senate-related triangle is analogous to the old game of "rocks, scissors, and paper." Filibusters trump a majority in the Senate, reconciliation trumps the filibuster, and the Byrd Rule trumps reconciliation.

The two triangles in figure 4.1 also allow us to array the various elements and their ancillary pieces by their offensive and defensive value in the legislative process. What stands out is the larger size of the defensive arsenal versus the offensive arsenal and how much of the defensive arsenal resides in the Senate, as shown in table 4.1.[4]

Each year, several hundred bills become law on average. A reconciliation bill becoming law is at best an annual event. Thus the filibuster and its impenetrable 41-vote barrier shape the daily proceedings of the Senate. This generates a different culture in the Senate than in the House. Higher degrees of consensus and bipartisanship are preconditions to passing controversial legislation in the Senate. Reconciliation, however, allows the majority of the Senate to once a year join with their ma-

Table 4.1. Offensive and Defensive Arsenals Residing in the House, Senate, and Presidency

Offensive Arsenal	Defensive Arsenal
House Rules Committee	Veto—presidency
Reconciliation—House and Senate	Filibuster—Senate Holds—Senate Nongermane amendments—Senate Byrd Rule—Senate Motion to recommit—House

jority colleagues in the House and pass far-reaching partisan legislation. But this is an exception to the Senate's normal operations. Thus, reconciliation is overwhelmingly a partisan tool, generally only used when both houses of Congress are controlled by the same party.[5]

 CHAPTER 5

Legislative Dynamics:
Strategic Options and Timing

Strategic Options and the
Rivers of Legislation

Contending parties enter the legislative arena with a wide range of purposes. For legislators, it is to exercise their craft, make their mark, and serve their constituents to achieve reelection. For the political parties, it is to capture control of the House of Representatives and Senate. For the president, it is to pursue his objectives either through cooperation or confrontation with Congress. For private parties—such as corporations, labor unions, public interest groups, and individuals—it is usually to achieve some narrow interest. These private interests speak the language of the public good and economic growth, but inevitably they have some narrow objective that they use the legislative process to achieve.[1]

In pursuing their interests, all parties use the full offensive and defensive arsenals already outlined. The obvious hope of everyone involved, and also of the general public, is that the collision of these competing interests, just like the economic marketplace or the judicial forum, will serve the public interest.

The participants in the legislative forum do not employ their legislative arsenals in a vacuum. Sound strategic choices and proper timing are essential, as with any human endeavor. I have found it fruitful—if hokey—to analogize the options in the legislative process to four rivers running from the North to South, dodging the Senate's "Icebergs" on the way to enactment. Figure 5.1 lays out these four options from the president's perspective. The same options are used by House and Senate sponsors of legislation. Ships laden with legislative cargo begin at the Presidential Port in the North Sea of Legislative Ambition, with their destination the Ocean of Legislative Tranquillity. Successful trips are celebrated on Rose Garden Island with awards of signing pens.

The Four Rivers of Legislation

The four rivers of legislation—Appropriations, Reconciliation, Tax and Entitlements, and Authorization—though familiar, all have different characteristics that make each journey unique. Choosing the correct river is the most important strategic choice that a sponsor of legislation can make. This admonition also applies to House and Senate sponsors of legislation. Knowing the tactics for properly navigating the unique characteristics of each river is how legislative practitioners make their living. Adopting a practitioner's perspective highlights the unique characteristics of each option. This perspective then assists us in properly assessing the American legislative process as an integrated whole. A brief summary follows of the strategic and tactical issues that confront any legislative journey down each river, seeking to avoid the Senate Iceberg and successfully reach the Ocean of Legislative Tranquillity.

The Reconciliation River

Look at figure 5.1. Only a masochist would not pick the Reconciliation River option if it were available. All the others have the Senate Iceberg, which can be lethal, impeding their path. Much of modern American legislative history has been about the reconciliation process. If you think about the "landmark" legislative issues over the past several decades, you would focus on President Ronald Reagan's 1981 spending cuts (which passed, 53–47, in the Senate), President Bill Clinton's 1993 deficit reduction package (51–50, with Vice President Al Gore breaking the tie), and President George W. Bush's 2001 tax cuts (51–50, with Vice President Dick Cheney's help). These were all reconciliation legislation. If you wanted to add the government shutdown led by Speaker of the House Newt Gingrich in 1995, or welfare reform in 1996, these were also in part reconciliation fights. Major exceptions would include Reagan's 1981 tax cuts, passed with the help of Southern Democrats in the

Figure 5.1. The Four Rivers of Legislation

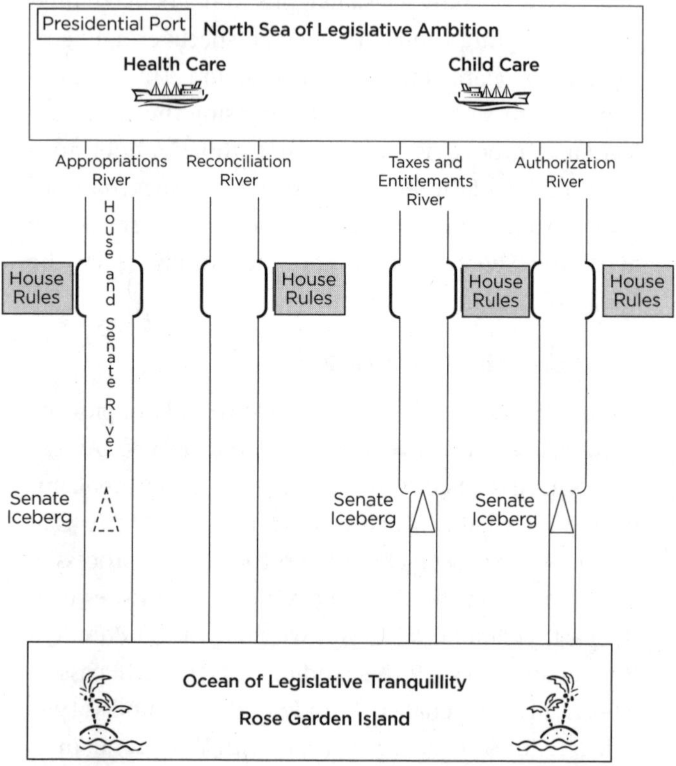

House and Senate, and the Medicare drug benefit passed in 2003 with a bitter House vote and a bipartisan fili-buster-proof majority of 61 votes in the Senate.

In introducing the notion of "landmark" legislation, I am employing a distinction between "landmark" and "important" legislation used intuitively by practitioners.

"Landmark" legislation consists of the sweeping, "signature" laws, noted above, by which a president's term is remembered. In the collective public memory, there are only two or three for any given presidential term. These are distinguished from "important" legislation, which leaves a mark but which, several years later, practitioners and the public have to strain to remember. Recent energy legislation in 2005 and 2007 would fit this description of "important." Both these laws, though "important," are not now remembered as "landmark" or "signature" legislation of the Bush administration comparable to the tax cuts of 2001. Moreover, during the course of their history, both energy bills were the subject of filibusters that required painstaking negotiations between the majority and minority in the Senate to pave the way for passage. In contrast to "landmark legislation," there are approximately a dozen "important" laws passed every Congress.[2]

Reconciliation, with its focus on taxes and entitlements, has been disproportionately responsible for the "landmark" legislation of the modern era. The votes in parentheses two paragraphs above also reinforce a point made above: Reconciliation is generally a deeply contested partisan process. Not one of the Senate vote counts noted above reached the 60-vote threshold to defeat a filibuster. For those hoping for a new era in the American legislative process, the question would be: Why can we not reach across the aisle and have the two parties agree to use the reconciliation process in a bipartisan fashion? A moment's reflection gives the answer. By announcing that they plan to employ the reconciliation process, a Senate majority is announcing in advance that it is not seeking minority input. The majority recognizes that the change is controversial, and it wants to eliminate the minority's leverage in the process that results from the threat of the filibuster and nongermane amendments. The minority's response is natural, human, and rational: You do not want our help, you will not get our help.

The Authorization River

The Authorization River is the principal waterway for most legislation, and the one we have been discussing with respect to the House Rules Committee, the Senate filibuster, and the presidential veto. All but three committees in the House and three in the Senate must travel down this river. Here they are subject to the Senate Iceberg. Also note how the river widens as it passes through the House Rules Committee.

The Taxes and Entitlements River

Article I, Section 7, of the Constitution provides that tax bills must start in the House, giving the House day-to-day leverage in its relations with the White House and the Senate that is rarely noted. Outside their constitutional mantle, tax bills that are not included in the reconciliation process are subject to the same risks of the Senate Iceberg as other legislation.

Entitlements are authorizations.[3] These are programs where anyone who fits a set of criteria is eligible for a benefit. For example, anyone over sixty-five years of age is eligible for Medicare and anyone over sixty-two is eligible for a Social Security benefit. Because the major entitlements, Medicare, and Social Security are under the jurisdiction of the same committees in the House (Ways and Means) and Senate (Finance) that write tax legislation, they have been grouped with taxes.[4] Like a tax bill, an entitlement bill is similar to other authorizations and subject to the Minority Tool Kit in the Senate. Because the entitlements are provided to anyone who is eligible, their costs are often called "uncontrollable." This is melodramatic. As the constitutional scholar Louis Fisher has noted, "The budget is controllable. Congress and the president simply choose to make it largely uncontrollable." Fisher goes on to explain that nothing prevents the president and Congress from changing these spending rules—nothing other than the fear of political retribution.[5]

This fear of political retribution is grounded in human nature. The federal government has promised the 80 million baby boomers who will soon receive Social Security and Medicare $40 to $50 trillion more than is presently available. Other entitlements—such as Medicaid, Veterans benefits, and federal pensions—will only add to the problem.

Less noted is the fact that all the industrial democracies are facing the same dilemma. In fact, Japan and Italy are presently experiencing more severe problems than the United States, while we are sliding toward trouble in the company of France, Germany, and Britain. Obviously, individual political systems and individual politicians are not the problem. Instead, wealthy industrial democracies are up against one of the strongest group of observed psychological traits in human nature. Humans hate to lose what they have and will fight fiercely to keep existing and promised benefits. In fact, humans consider existing benefits twice as valuable as possible future gains. This "loss aversion" provides a powerful status quo bias to democratic political processes. This does not make entitlement reform hopeless, but it does mean that American democracy is in for a multiyear, probably multidecade, struggle to align its commitments and resources at the federal level. It should also serve as a warning against the usual cadre of political and policy pied pipers offering quick and painless solutions.[6]

The Appropriations River

Appropriations are like the pony express—they always get through. The cash these bills contains is the lifeblood of American government. Included in these bills are funding for national defense, highways, education, prisons, and community health centers. Although subject to the filibuster, appropriations bills have de facto procedural options that approach reconciliation, including limitations on nongermane amendments. No one shoots the payroll clerk.[7]

A close look at the Appropriations River would look like figure 5.2, which reflects the fact that the appropriations process has carved alternative channels around

Figure 5.2. The Appropriations River

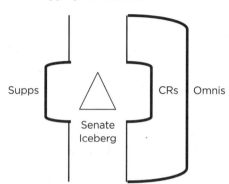

Note: Supps = supplementals; CRs = continuing resolutions; Omnis = omnibus bills.

prospective Senate filibusters.[8] The three key channels are noted here.

The first alternative channel is continuing resolutions (CRs). In the event one or several appropriations bills are behind schedule, Congress can pass a CR, which is designed to maintain federal funding for programs at the existing level until the proper appropriations bill is enacted into law. (Because CRs are laws like any other, occasionally legislative mischief pops up on them.)

The second alternative channel is omnibus bills (omnis). At the end of the legislative session, if several of the twelve appropriations bill are tied up in parliamentary maneuvers, they can be wrapped into a single large package called an omnibus appropriations bill. Each year, some combination of CRs and omnis are now the general rule, rather than the exception. Only twice in the past thirty years have all the appropriations bills been passed on time before the end of the fiscal year.

The third alternative channel is supplementals (supps). Like any business or household, the federal government has unforeseen expenses. Hurricanes, floods, military operations, or even war are the most predictable of these "unforeseen events." To address these contingencies, Congress passes supps to augment funds already provided in the regular appropriations bills. The unstated trick of a supplemental is that because it is passed after the fiscal year has already started and is declared an "emergency," it is outside the normal scrutiny and machinery of the budgetary process. In short, supps provide free money. This is a temptation for members of Congress, who occasionally load up supps with projects that might not otherwise pass scrutiny. Supps are also a temptation for presidents. Most of the war in Iraq has been funded by the supps process, and not through the regular appropriations process. Free money or not, these are real dollars and count against the deficit.

Time and the Concept of "Carrying Capacity"

The legislative process—with its three-party negotiations between the House, Senate, and president—takes time. Years, and, in the case of the Medicare drug benefit, decades are consumed in passing a particular piece of legislation.

Beneath the surface chop and froth of the legislative process, there are predictable temporal cycles that significantly affect the prospects for the passage of legislation. The most obvious is the electoral cycle. Every two years, the full House and one-third of the Senate are up for reelection. A new president is elected every fourth year. Legislation must be passed during the two years between elections. Toward the end of the second year, two contradictory processes occur. In anticipation of the elections, members of Congress begin to shy away from controversial votes. Sponsors of legislation, however, begin to behave like salmon swimming upstream to spawn and redouble their efforts to pass bills they have sponsored before Congress ends. The two parties also begin maneuvering toward the end of the two-year cycle to try and schedule votes that will enhance the electoral chances of their respective sides before the elections. Superimposed on this situation is the fact that, invariably, many of the appropriations bills remain unfinished at the end of the second year. These conflicting forces guarantee a volatile legislative and political stew in the last months before the elections. A large portion of managing this process is the simple recognition that it is coming.

Earlier in the book, Senator John Sherman in 1865 was quoted on how the Senate abandoned the effort to readmit Louisiana after the Civil War in order to pass appropriations bills at the end of the legislative session. From its inception, the filibuster has had its most powerful effect at the end of a session. It completely alters the balance of power in the Senate. In the last months of a legislative session during an election year, the minority, using its Minority Tool Kit, gains control of the Senate, and thus of the entire legislative process.

It is one of the ironies of the legislative process that the minority party, which invariably claims that the majority has run a "do-nothing Congress," in fact has the power to ensure that the claim is at least partially true. Of equal significance is that the minority, by using its Minority Tool Kit throughout the year, can set an overall limit on the amount of legislation the Senate can process in a year. This notion of an overall limit, or "legislative carrying capacity," over a one- or two-year congressional cycle has consequences for those who argue for a more activist legislative agenda.

To appreciate the elements in this shift in power, let us examine in more detail a typical election year. Table 5.1 is the Senate calendar for such a year. It is apparent that after July, the congressional calendar is compressed. Major legislation that is not passed by September runs a substantial risk that it will not survive the September crunch before Congress adjourns in October for the November elections.

With these basics in place, let us look at the actual re-election year of 2004 in the Senate (my last year working in the Senate), as shown in table 5.2. In 2003, Congress passed and the president signed a bitterly contested Medicare drug bill. Conservatives in the House and liberals in the Senate almost defeated it. Going into 2004,

Table 5.1. The Senate Calendar for an Election Year

Month	Event
January	President's State of the Union Address
February	President's budget submitted
March	Legislative hearings
April	Legislative hearings and committee markups
May	Markups
June	Congressional primaries
July	House and Senate floor action
August	Vacation
September	Crunch: election-year legislative rush and Appropriations Conference Report crush
October	Congress adjourns to campaign
November	Elections
December	

the majority leadership in both the House and Senate planned a lean legislative agenda to avoid internal controversy before the fall elections. For the Senate side, the Republicans listed their priorities as shown in table 5.2; I have put some comments in the right-hand column to give context.[9] To have any relation to reality, the schedule required continuous updating. The general planning cycle for the majority proceeded as follows—and the minority had a similar cycle:

Monday, 11:00 AM: Full leadership staff planning meeting.
Monday, 3:00 PM: Senate majority leadership meeting.
Monday, 5:00 PM: Meeting of the committee chairmen.
Tuesday, 12:30 PM: Policy lunch with all Republican senators.
Friday, 11:00 AM: Meeting of the majority leader's staff to update the plan for following week.

Table 5.2. Republican Senate Legislative Priorities for the Actual Reelection Year 2004

Bill	Comments
CRITICAL PATH	
Omnis	These holdover appropriation bills needed to be passed in early 2004.
Highways	We expected this to pass. The Democrats eventually decided to wait and see if a Kerry presidency would give them a better deal.
Corporate tax (FSC/ETI)	This took three cloture tries and did not pass until early October.
Debt limit	
Appropriations	
POSSIBLE	
Immigration	No critical mass ever developed.
Reconciliation	Debt limit, death tax, extenders. Did not happen. The Senate majority of 51–49 was too fractured over need for new tax cuts.
CLOTURE	
Asbestos	We knew these items would require cloture. We expected class action, guns, and Internet tax to pass. All failed.
Class action	
Guns	
Medical malpractice	
Internet tax	
Judges	
CONSTITUTIONAL AMENDMENTS	
Victims' rights	
Flag burning	
Gay marriage	

The preceding sets us up to discuss the fall crunch in 2004. By late July, the Senate majority leadership had targeted these priorities for September:

PRIORITIES
Judges
Homeland Security appropriations
Flag-burning amendment
Tax conference (extenders, etc.).

CHALLENGES
Appropriations
9/11 Intelligence reform legislation (the 9/11 Commission reported its recommendations during the year. The legislation passed the Senate in the fall, and it was eventually signed by the president in early 2005).

The actual calendar for our activities for September 2004 closely matched the July priority list, except for one notable omission: the flag-burning amendment. What happened? Senator Tom Daschle (D-S.D.), the minority leader of the Senate, had a straightforward response to our July priorities: We will work with you on everything except the flag-burning amendment. In fact, if you bring it up, you will pass nothing for the month. This triggered a typical and heated discussion as to whether the minority leader was bluffing, and what were the political risks and rewards of such a confrontation, particularly with the fall elections two months away. The final decision to pass our other priorities and accede to Senator Daschle's demand was for me the correct one. But it also highlights the point that at the end of the legislative session, before an election, the minority in the Senate is in control, easily able to frustrate not only its majority colleagues in the Senate but also the House majority and the president.

This Daschle vignette makes a point and raises a question. The point relates to "carrying capacity." As the discussion of 2004 makes clear, Senate passage is the obvious limiting factor for the entire legislation process. Those who are concerned about "gridlock" must as a matter of consistency urge elimination of the Senate filibuster and other elements of the Senate Iceberg.

Some scholars who look at the Senate in these "polarized," "hyperpartisan" times consider it a "deeper puzzle" that as ugly as it is to watch, any substantial work gets done at all.[10] This leads to the question that in light of Senator Daschle's leverage at the end of 2004, why did he allow anything to pass? Why not a scorched-earth September? The answer is the key to the Senate, the American legislative machine, and a partial refutation of recent breast-beating. The American legislative machine is a shared system.[11] No one wants to blow it up. Members are out to make a career—hopefully a distinguished one. Competing parties want to gain control of the system; but once in charge, they want a machine that will give them results. Each side also knows that because there is always another election coming in two years, there is nothing that could be considered a "final victory." Once in power, they must maintain power by keeping the trust and support of the electorate. This requires them to demonstrate mature leadership. Thus, within this shared system, each side maneuvers for advantage but remains beholden to the electorate for continuing control.

Senator Daschle was well aware of all this. He wanted to gain seats in the Senate for his party by demonstrating leadership. He also wanted to eliminate election-year votes called by the majority that put his Democratic colleagues at a disadvantage. He knew skillful maneuvering was essential. He also knew that a scorched-earth September would be political suicide.

 CHAPTER 6

Performance and Parties

Performance

As we enter our concluding phase, where I will offer some judgments, it is worth sounding the alarm over the excessive use of code words. Few Americans want a government stuck in gridlock, irrevocably divided by crazed bands of hyperpolarized partisans. Most Americans, however, would favor a government that provides them with policy stability relying on a healthy two-party system that allows for principled opposition through the full and free expression of new ideas. Table 6.1 provides a ready reference to the competing code words used by contending factions in public debate over the American legislative system. For convenience's sake, I have labeled the two competing schools of thought "Doom and Gloom" and "What, Me Worry?" On the left, I have listed

Table 6.1. The Two Competing Schools of Thought in Public Debate over the American Legislative System

Doom and Gloom		What, Me Worry?
Gridlock	=	Policy stability
Partisanship	=	Competitive two-party system
Polarization	=	Party unity, principled opposition

the code words used by the Doom and Gloom school to describe the American legislative process. On the right, I have listed an alternative characterization for each code word. Certainly, the left-hand side of the debate has prevailed in the public mind. We need to also be candid enough to recognize that we are entering an area of subjective bias and fervently held personal opinion. The prospect of either side completely convincing the other is remote.

In an effort to skirt some of this problem, so far we have attempted to lay out the practitioners' viewpoint as a platform from which to analyze the debate. The first part of this effort has been to give a fuller and more accurate description of how America's legislative machine actually operates. Moreover, this legislative machine has been evolving through much of American history. Neither the intensity of modern debates in the House of Representatives nor the deliberate pace of some Senate deliberations is new. The House, with its Rules Committee, and the Senate, with the filibuster, began in the nineteenth century to establish procedures tailored to each body. These procedures, together with the president's powers, now constitute the modern American legislative system.

This conclusion, based on examining the respective histories of the House Rules Committee and the Senate filibuster, undercuts to some degree the breathless prose of the Doom and Gloom school that today's legislative difficulties are unprecedented in American history. It does not, however, refute the contention that political partisanship and polarization may have increased since the 1970s. The fact that scholars have established that the late nineteenth century was even more polarized and partisan than today does no more than provide perspective.[1] Each generation must address its own problems. The question remains whether the polarization and partisanship of today, though not unique, is substantially degrading our ability to address the salient issues facing America.[2]

All this is by way of easing into the slippery issue of evaluating the performance of the modern American legislative system. Quality and quantity are the two obvious criteria for evaluating legislative performance. Occasionally, a brave commentator will claim that the quality of legislation has declined as Congress has become more polarized and partisan. Cited as proof is the rush of legislation passed by Newt Gingrich and a new Republican majority in the House in the first hundred days of the session in 1995. But this thesis suffers from the fatal example of the quality of legislation passed by President Lyndon Johnson in 1964. As his biographer

Doris Kearns Goodwin noted, President Johnson during this period practiced the "politics of haste," in which "solutions were often devised and rushed into law before the problems were understood."[3]

For practitioners, the claim that the technical quality of legislation of one era is better than another's falls on deaf ears. All of us regale each other with tales of the flaws in our own legislative efforts. I will spare the reader my stockpile of stories and end this discussion on quality with de Tocqueville's prescient observation that a democracy's laws "are almost always defective and untimely."[4]

Quantity is a different matter. Here there is a definitive work, David Mayhew of Yale's *Divided We Govern*. Mayhew has looked at the quantity of "important" legislation (in contrast to the "landmark" legislation discussed under reconciliation) from 1945 to 2002. Although focused on the issue of the impact of divided government on the production of critical legislation, this period coincides with the claimed increase in partisanship and polarization during the post–World War II era. The clear conclusion of Mayhew's work is that divided government, and increased polarization and partisanship, have not decreased the passage of "important" legislation by Congress. In short, the legislative machine is an all-weather machine, able to produce legislative product regardless of abrupt and severe changes in the political climate. There are ebbs and flows, but overall the American version of the legislative machine keeps churning out product.[5]

Table 6.2 takes Mayhew's work and puts it in tabular form for important bills passed since 1945. Within these numbers, there is room for a great deal of quibbling. One point that stands out is that the administrations of Johnson, Richard Nixon, and Gerald Ford, spanning 1965 to 1976, were a period of record legislative output. The consensus explanation, and a plausible one at that, is that during this period of social ferment, groups representing blacks, consumers, environmentalists, and women, among others, all entered the legislative arena with pent-up lists of demands requiring national attention. Thus, although President Johnson initiated the legislative outpouring, the natural momentum of these phenomena continued through the Nixon and Ford presidencies. During these three presidential terms, 121 new federal social programs were initiated, along with 9 new federal agencies. Spending on social programs at the federal, state, and local levels rose from 11.2 percent of gross national product in 1965 to 19.3 percent at the end of President Ford's term.[6] This legislative outpouring set the stage for the conservative backlash of the early 1980s.

There was also a sudden surge of legislative activity after 9/11 in the 2001–2 time frame. The question could be raised of whether the response to a crisis should be counted. But as Mayhew accurately notes, crises in American history have repeatedly led to legislative surges, such as Franklin Delano Roosevelt's response in the 1930s to the Great Depression or Johnson's legislative response to the Kennedy assassination. Responding to

Table 6.2. The Quantity of "Important" Legislation according to David Mayhew's Work, 1945–2002

Years	First Session	Second Session	Total	Government Control
1945–48		10		Democratic, 1945–47; divided, 1947–49
1949–52	12	6	18	Democratic
1953–56	9	6	15	Republican, 1953–55; divided, 1955–57
1957–60	11	5	16	Divided
1961–64	15	13	28	Democratic
1965–68	22	16	38	Democratic
1969–72	22	16	38	Divided
1973–76	22	14	36	Divided
1977–80	12	10	22	Democratic
1981–84	9	7	16	Divided
1985–88	9	12	21	Divided
1989–92	9	8	17	Divided
1993–96	12	15	27	Democratic, 1993–95; divided, 1995–97
1997–2000	9	6	15	Divided
2001–2	15			Divided

Source: David Mayhew, *Divided We Govern: Policy Control, Lawmaking, and Investigations, 1946–1990,* 2nd ed. (New Haven, Conn.: Yale University Press, 2005).

Note: The breakdown of the divided governments is as follows: Democratic control of the presidency and Republican control of both houses of Congress, 1947–49 and 1995–2001; Republican control of the presidency and Democratic control of both houses of Congress, 1955–61, 1969–77, and 1987–93; Republican control of the presidency and the Senate and Democratic control of the House, 1981–87; Republican control of the presidency and the House and Democratic control of the Senate 2001–3.

crises is one of the hallmarks of the American legislative system.[7]

The most recent review of the modern legislative process confirms Mayhew's basic point that the modern American legislative machine, regardless of the political environment in which it operates, continues to churn out product at a relatively constant rate. As Galston and Nivola noted in 2006:

> Whatever else the overall legislative record of recent years may show, sclerosis has not been a distinguishing characteristic. Reform of the welfare system, substantial tax reductions, big trade agreements, a great expansion of federal intervention in local public education, important course correction in foreign policy, reorganization of the intelligence bureau, significant campaign finance law, new rules governing bankruptcy and class-action litigation, a huge new cabinet department, massive enlargement of Medicare—for better or worse, all these milestones and others, were achieved despite polarized politics.[8]

Mayhew's conclusions "rattled students of Congress and the presidency."[9] Since then, proponents of the Doom and Gloom school have been, in the words of Southern folklore, "squirming like worms on a hot rock." Because these proponents decry the rise in polarization and partisanship, they are unable to accept the fact that the American legislation machine, like a ship in a rough seas, appears to bob along in these polarized and partisan waters, making steady progress, occasionally taking on water, and refusing to follow the fervent hopes of its critics that it sink.

A moment's reflection would give the reason for this durability. The American legislative process is not a recent invention. Its present configuration is the result of over a century of legislative evolution. In fact, as noted above, the late nineteenth century was more partisan and polarized than today. Thus, the American legislative process has seen all this before. Along the way, it has survived a civil war, the assassination of four presidents, two world wars, and the Great Depression. Just listing the traumas of the 1960s and 1970s—widespread race riots; the assassinations of President John F. Kennedy, Senator Robert Kennedy, and Martin Luther King; defeat in Vietnam with 50,000 killed; and Watergate—provides important perspective for our own era.

This durability is also woven into the design of the legislative machine. Both the House and Senate have created institutional responses to fluctuations in partisanship and polarization. In the House, the machine is designed to pass legislation that suits the majority. The degree of separation between the majority and minority, the definition of polarization, is irrelevant. The majority is not looking to the minority for help in passing its program. It expects to provide all the votes necessary from its side.[10]

The Senate has adopted the opposite response. In light of the filibuster, and with the exception of the reconciliation process (or perhaps an overwhelming partisan majority), major legislation must have a bipartisan coalition to pass.[11] Thus, both branches of Congress have fashioned specific procedures over time that represent strategic responses to fluctuations in the polarization and partisanship of their own membership and the electorate. These responses allow for significant legislation to continue to pass the House and Senate, regardless of the level of polarization and partisanship in the country. It is tempting to say that the unique responses of each chamber of Congress have conferred on them a form of legislative immunity to increased polarization. The Doom and Gloom school ignores this point. Mayhew's analysis represents a testament to the durability and flexibility of the legislative machine over time. As the sportscasters tell us every weekend, winning ugly still counts as a win.[12]

By considering Mayhew's analysis in combination with the description earlier in this book of the legislative machine's unique elements, we can discern the five major legislative realities of the modern American legislative system:

1. The House with its Rules Committee is designed for legislative offense. It invariably moves first in the legislative process. The winner-take-all ethic of the House means that the minority has little leverage in the legislative process. Historically, most of the interesting emotional fireworks occur in the House.

2. The Senate filibuster and other minority tactics make the Senate the prospective choke point in the American legislative process. As long as the minority has 41 votes, it has equal leverage with the majority in the Senate. This means that bipartisan negotiations

are generally a precondition to passing contentious legislation in the Senate. These bipartisan negotiations leave their imprint on legislation sent to the president. This allows for bipartisan, but incremental, progress through the American legislative process.

3. The exception in the Senate to the barrier posed by a minority filibuster is budget reconciliation. This process allows the majority, generally once a year, to pass sweeping budget legislation with 51 votes. These reconciliation bills are, with few exceptions, highly partisan.

4. Thus, the American legislative system can provide for either incremental bipartisan progress or sweeping partisan progress.

5. Item 4, the basic conclusion of this study, has one obvious exception: political crises. As noted by Mayhew, the filibuster is a strategic option available to the minority in the Senate to advance its political or policy interests. It is not used for political suicide missions.[13]

The legislative reality that the American system can provide negotiated incremental bipartisan progress, or sweeping partisan reform, but not both, presents a problem for the proponents of "postpartisan" politics. At present, there is no gear in the legislative machine to produce sweeping bipartisan change. Those looking for a new era in American politics might be willing to admit this shortcoming in the present system. The question then becomes whether there is either a fix for the existing machine or a blueprint available for a new machine.

Parties

Against the cries of "polarization" and "hyperpartisanship," the "What, Me Worry" school has continued to ask, what is the problem? Certainly, it cannot be the existence of political parties. It is virtually impossible to contemplate a modern democracy without parties. The fact that the parties have become stronger and more cohesive is to be expected. Certainly the existence of political and legislative competition cannot be considered a problem.[14] These are baked in the bread of any democratic system. The fact that Americans have only two parties and not Israel's thirteen or Italy's thirty-two is a blessing. Moreover, scholars are telling us that our present bout of polarization and partisanship in America is "mild" by historical standards. In 2008, America's two parties were shrilly arguing over whether to *increase* a program for children's health (known as SCHIP) by $5 billion versus $30 billion over the next five years. Parties in other countries are killing each other in large numbers over religious, ethnic, and power disputes. Again, what is the problem?

Certainly it would be easy to dismiss the central thesis of the Doom and Gloom school. Much of its analysis consists of comparing today's legislative process with that of the 1950s and 1960s. In its view, civility and comity reigned during this era. People of goodwill amiably settled their differences in this "Age of Bargaining." National issues were settled in a bipartisan fashion "during this golden age of statesmanship and cooperation."[15]

In forwarding this "golden age fallacy"[16] line of argument, its proponents are opening themselves up to several fatal lines of attack. First, this is the same legislative period that Burns denounces in his *Deadlock of Democracy,* and during which others began to question whether America needed such a "relic" as the Senate.[17]

Second, and more troubling, is putting a halo on an age where the national legislature was the principal point of leverage in the South's continuing effort to maintain a racist, segregated regime in the states of the original Confederacy. In 1959, the South had two-thirds of the chairmanships in the House and three-fifths in the Senate. William White's classic study of the Senate, *The Citadel,* provides a favorable view of the courtliness and civility of the Southern chairmen who ran the Senate. But he did admit that the Senate was "the South's unending revenge upon the North for Gettysburg."[18] It is easy to forget that through the late 1950s and into the early 1960s, blacks were still being lynched in the South.

It is easy to wax self-righteous on this issue, so let me just finish with a quotation from Senator James Eastland, the chairman of the Senate Judiciary Committee, responsible for civil rights legislation during the "Golden Age." In 1956, while blacks marched in the Montgomery, Alabama, bus boycott, Senator Eastland addressed a crowd of 10,000 at a White Citizens Council rally in the Montgomery Coliseum:

> In every stage of the bus boycott we have been op-
> pressed and degraded because of black, slimy, juicy, un-
> bearable stinking niggers, . . . African flesh-eaters. When
> in the course of human events it becomes necessary to
> abolish the Negro race, proper methods should be used.
> Among these are guns, bows and arrows, slingshots and
> knives. . . . All whites are created equal and with certain
> rights, among these are life, liberty and the pursuit of
> dead niggers.[19]

Those concerned over the consequences of polarization and "hyperpartisanship" are longtime students of
American government and recognize the weaknesses in
their arguments. The question remains whether, at
some primal emotional level, they were simply suffer-
ing partisan unease at Republican control of the House
and Senate from 1994 through 2006, which vanished
with the 2006 and 2008 elections, or are there still fundamental reasons for concern.[20] My view is they are
onto something—they just do not know what.

Ronald Brownstein's *The Second Civil War* is the most
articulate expression of these concerns, which he calls
the Great Sorting Out, and which has two themes:

1. Southern Democrats in the late 1950s and 1960s
   shifted to the Republican Party, with a corresponding
   shift of liberal eastern Republicans into the Democratic party.[21] This transformed the Democratic Party
   into a liberal party based in the East and on the West
   Coast (blue states) and the Republican Party into a
   conservative party in the South and West (red states).
   The Midwest then became the battleground between

the parties for dominance. Thus, the two parties, both of which had liberal and conservative wings in the 1950s, were transformed into ideologically and geographically unified parties.

2. In addition to geographic and ideological unity, the parties are becoming more culturally uniform. Married couples and churchgoers are more likely to be Republican, while single, secular Americans are more likely to vote Democratic. (Brownstein does admit that beneath this trend are the positive trends of a more tolerant America on race and sex and less class division between the parties.)

In Brownstein's view, this combination of electoral trends is "dissolving the political incentives that encouraged cooperation."[22]

In addition, Brownstein is clearly taken aback by the "gleeful ferocity of thousands of partisan blogs."[23] Although he accords Republicans the lion's share of the blame for the state of American political discourse, he is unsettled by attending the yearly convention of the liberal Democratic Web site the *DailyKos*, home of the "Kossacks," where the loudest catcalls were not for Republicans but "Neville Chamberlain Democrats" who were cooperating with Republicans.[24]

The reform proposals of Brownstein and his fellow critics follow a general pattern: (1) Attacking the present legislative process as dysfunctional; (2) waxing nostalgic for the lost golden era of the 1950s and 1960s; and

(3) forwarding a set of proposals, such as open primaries, to elect a new type of centrist politician.

Although rhetorically inspiring, this package of proposals is destined for, in Trotsky's words, "the dustbin of history." The emotional impact of these proposals comes from their urging all Americans to rise above their parochial and political interests and cooperate. This is, in fact, how Americans respond in a crisis, but it is not a sound basis for the day-to-day task of politics to resolve strongly held and conflicting claims. It overlooks both the strengths and weaknesses of the American party system. It also ignores human nature.

Let us promptly dispose of these proposals so we can move on to more serious matters. First, the bulk of this study has been devoted to the proposition that the American legislative machine is a flexible, adaptable process that Mayhew and my fellow practitioners have correctly noted wins ugly. Critics of the legislative process have focused on some insult of the day in the House, where the majority routinely abuses the minority. As noted above, this narrow focus misses how the overall system manages to produce legislation through a wide range of political conditions. Second, the nostalgia for the 1950s and 1960s is an example of "memory polishing history" that cannot stand any disciplined scrutiny.[25] Finally, I am agnostic on open primaries. But when the conservative talk show host Rush Limbaugh gleefully launched "Operation Chaos" and urged Republicans and Independents to vote for Senator Hillary Clinton in the 2008 Indiana primary to disrupt Senator Barack Obama's drive for the Democratic presidential nomination, this undoubtedly was a setback for those urging open primaries for federal, state, and local elections.

Parties as the Basic Unit of Cooperation

What the Doom and Gloom school is trying to avoid is the fundamental truth of American politics: The basic unit of cooperation in American politics is the party. "The political parties created democracy" and "modern democracy is unthinkable save in term of the parties."[26] The critics wisely do not dispute this statement, even though they spend a lot of time wriggling around on their hot rock trying to avoid the force of it.

Its truth is also supported by the science of human nature. Early on, Darwin noted that the virtues of courage, sympathy, and unselfishness would tend to proliferate because "a tribe possessing the above qualities in a high degree would spread and be victorious over other tribes."[27] This observation has been distilled to the conclusion among evolutionary biologists that humans "cooperate to compete."[28] One of the most recent applications of this insight to politics is found in the British behavioral scientist Robert Hinde's 2007 book *Bending the Rules*. Hinde lays out how cooperative, cohesive groups outperform their more selfish competitors. Accordingly, many of our moral virtues that foster cooperation arose from an "in-group" moral code as part of "intergroup" competition. "And for the politician at every level, party loyalty, a form of group loyalty based in a long history of biological and cultural evolution, has come to be seen as a moral issue."[29] Hinde's insight explains why all Americans can join together to face opponents from overseas, but why we revert to party loyalty for domestic political contests.[30] (No one likes a traitor or a snitch.)

Hinde also sees the same downside to this phenomenon as Brownstein saw at the *DailyKos* convention. The moral code of cooperating in a group is enforced by "the terrible demon of moral rectitude" against in-group defectors.[31] Parties with their in-group loyalty are a fact of American politics—and a fact of human nature.[32]

Parties and the Great American Consensus

Not only is the party the unit of cooperation in American politics, but, as John Hilley noted, the energy for American democracy also comes from the parties. The parties also play an important policy role. There is a vast literature in the political science community on this. Interestingly, the best exposition comes from a philosopher, Harvard's Robert Nozick:

> The task for a party that leaves power and moves into opposition is not to repeat its previous position unchanged but to observe with some understanding and even sympathy the pursuit of other goals worthy enough to move a considerable portion of the electorate,

and meanwhile to articulate its own vision, building upon old or even new goals it feels a special kinship with, in time helping the public to formulate its vision of the next zag. In any case, given the choice between permanently institutionalizing the particular content of any group of political principles thus far articulated . . . and the zigzag process of democratic politics. . . . I'll vote for the zigzag every time.[33]

This is obviously a mouthful, but it saves a long exegesis on the value of parties. It also shows how a zigzagging electorate, like a fickle consumer, can keep a tight leash on the parties, moving them in and out of power as it suits its purposes. It also shows how parties out of power can retool their programs to meet not only the electorate's needs of today but also its hopes for tomorrow.

The thrust and parry of this two-party competition can be seen in the policy arena in Congress as the parties invade their opponent's turf with new proposals and defend their own turf against the other side. Over time, in response to Republican incursions, the Democrats passed welfare reform (1996), supported comprehensive criminal justice reform (1994, 1996), and created a budgetary surplus during President Bill Clinton's second term. The Republicans, in turn, passed educational reform in the No Child Left Behind legislation (2001), and the Medicare prescription drug bill (2003) after thwarting Democratic efforts to do the same for decades. Writing in early 2009, there is little doubt that the Democrats are close to successfully grinding down Republican opposition, and it is only a matter of time before some form of universal health coverage, probably subsidized coverage through the private sector, becomes the law of the land. (I do not believe I am alone in wondering whether we can afford it.)[34]

This favorable treatment of the thrust and parry of competing parties in the legislative arena, and its intellectual support by Nozick, is at odds with the widespread notion in the popular media, highlighted by Brownstein and others, that the American political system has been rendered dysfunctional by differences between the parties. Part of this perception is Michael Kinsey's astute observation that the media has a vested economic interest in "sowing serial social panic."[35] But there is also something more at play. Interestingly, David Frum, a former *Forbes* magazine reporter and White House speechwriter under President George W. Bush, notes in his recent book that as the "substantive policy differences between the parties shrank between 1995 and 2005, . . . the two parties seethed in rage at each other."[36]

From the other side of the political aisle, Hilley supports Frum's observation by noting that "although partisan competition for office is at the core of our political system," over the long run "our vibrant, messy, contested, but fundamentally open and fair form of government has allowed the American people to steer their ship of state, deal with new challenges and overcome many differences of belief and opinion." In fact this competitive system has produced a "positive and expansive American consensus." For Hilley, the current American consensus consists of

> free citizens who are secure in our fundamental rights; we should be secure as a nation and in our persons and possessions; we should have an open and competitive economy that rewards work and fair play; the doors of education should be open to everyone as the gateway to opportunity; we should live in a clean and safe environment; we should guarantee that our seniors, the disabled, and those who have sacrificed for country have access to the basic essentials of life; and we should provide a safety net for the poor, as well as the tools they need to lift themselves out of poverty. This American consensus did not did not spring forth full grown, . . . [but was] made possible by the serendipitous combination of economic growth, the goodness of a free people and our competitive politics.[37]

Because Hilley is on a roll, we will let him finish:

> Political competition has been a prime catalyst propelling the values, ideas and policies through which the American consensus has emerged. And that progress has been contentious. . . . Partisan competition has been at the center of our struggle to advance as a people and a nation. It has been our most important engine for adaptation and change—one that remains in full motion.[38]

Integrating the previous discussion provides us with figure 6.1, which illustrates how this American consensus is achieved. Among the myriad factors, including the well-recognized role of elections, are two lesser-noted but critical elements: the maneuvering by the compet-

Figure 6.1. The Competitive Party Cycle and the Great American Consensus

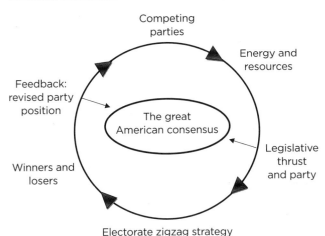

Electorate zigzag strategy

ing parties in the legislative process in fleshing out and publicizing party proposals; and the revision of party positions following each election as the parties adapt to the new legislative realities brought on by the elections. Parts of this process can be unsightly, such as the thrust and parry between the parties in the legislative forum that is often called "squabbling." But it is an essential part of the process of advancing new policy options and generating the American consensus.[39]

The Dark Side of Parties

At this juncture, the reader could properly call foul. Before critiquing the solutions offered by Brownstein and others and then bludgeoning the reader with long quotations from Nozick and Hilley (don't you have any ideas of your own, Rawls?), I noted that Brownstein and others were onto something; they just did not know what.

What Brownstein and others are signaling is a threat, not a present reality, to the Madisonian system of the separation of powers. Put simply, do modern parties, which are now regionally homogenous, ideologically uniform, and culturally similar, when they are combined with the technological firepower provided by the Internet, Web-based vigilantes, modern information processing technology, large-scale data manipulation, message discipline, extensive media expertise, and the access to billions of dollars, represent a threat to the separation of powers fundamental to the Constitution?[40] And is this threat augmented by the ongoing division of the media, both electronic and print, along partisan lines?

The scholars speak of the parties as "bridging" the Madisonian system. This is often stated in a favorable context of parties constructively providing needed bridges to the various elements of the Constitution's separation of powers system. This misses the psychological intent of the parties. The parties are not out to provide constructive bridges for the Madisonian system. They are out to hijack the Madisonian system. Their dream is to leap the barriers in the Constitution and to put control of the entire federal government under one unified command structure.[41]

Here, figures 6.2 and 6.3 are worth several thousand words, and I will spare the reader my full exegesis on the *Federalist* papers (which remains available upon request). Figure 6.2 shows the Madisonian system. Fearing that the "facility and excess of lawmaking seem to be diseases to which our governments are most liable," the Founders decided to employ a system of separation of powers under which "ambition must be made to counteract ambition."[42] Figure 6.3 shows how each party, unified, seeks to enact its agenda. But enacting the full agenda requires controlling the entire federal system, including the judiciary. The thrust and resources for this effort come from the full range of partisan interest groups, political and economic. This is no "bridging" operation. This is an assault seeking full control. Honest partisans will admit to this goal. These two figures make the case for the validity of Brownstein's fears (he just lacks my artistic skills). This tension between party and the Madisonian system is a long-standing risk in American politics. Whether in this century Brownstein's fears

Figure 6.2. The Madisonian System: Ambition Counteracts Ambition

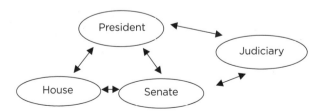

Figure 6.3. The Partisan Assault Schematic: How Each Party Seeks to Enact Its Agenda

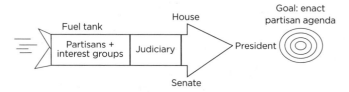

will fully materialize, it is too early to tell. But it is not too early to contemplate the risk.

The Filibuster to the Rescue

The reason for the diversion here from the legislative process into the dynamics of America's political parties is that the only barrier to Brownstein's nightmare is the Senate minority's ability to filibuster, and thus force bipartisan negotiations. Without the filibuster, the only stumbling block to full partisan control of the American legislative system would be internal party divisions. These divisions should fade because, as Brownstein properly notes, modern parties are becoming more disciplined and unified.

Thus, we find that the Holy Grail of bipartisanship demands the presence of the Senate filibuster. Critics have noted that the type of hard bargaining in the Senate that produces bipartisan legislation slows down the rate at which legislation passes (thus, my notion of carrying capacity). Even though some scholars who have examined the modern American legislative process have to date found hard bargaining, but not gridlock (Mayhew, Sinclair, and Galston and Nivola), it doesn't mean that the filibuster doesn't slow down the legislative process and pose a risk of gridlock. So far in American history, the fact that the legislative process is a shared system that the parties separately want to control, but not destroy, has allowed for a form of steady, incremental progress that has left both partisans and impatient commentators dissatisfied. Those commentators who have pleaded for an end to gridlock so that the nation can achieve rapid bipartisan change have missed the fundamental tension in the American legislative process. Rapid policy change, other than in the national response to a crisis, is achieved through the partisanship of the reconciliation process or large partisan majorities. Thus, the legislative machinery available for rapid policy change is mostly partisan. Bipartisan change means time-consuming incremental change through hard negotiations by a Senate majority with a Senate minority armed with the filibuster and the rest of the Minority Tool Kit. The two goals of the public mind—ending gridlock through rapid and fundamental change, and ending polarization through large bipartisan coalitions, both of which have been fostered by the commentators—are incompatible with the present workings of the modern American legislative machine.

Advocates of "postpartisan" politics invoke a new era where these tensions dissolve. Regrettably, as we have shown, the existing legislative machine will not grant them their wish. Moreover, as long as political parties remain the unit of cooperation within the American political system—and it is difficult to imagine American democracy without them—the desire of the "postpartisans" to cross the River Jordan into the political promised land will remain unfulfilled. More important, the "postpartisans" fail to realize that the clash of contending forces they hear in the political arena is the sound of democracy at work.

 CHAPTER 7

Prospects

Filibusters and Parties

Neither political parties nor the filibuster are found in the Constitution.[1] They are the two great mutations in the American legislative system. As we have seen, there is also a tension between them. Political parties provide the electorate with the energy and policy choices essential to democratic deliberation. But these same parties are out to circumvent the checks and balances of the Constitution by capturing the full machinery of the federal government and using it to enact a partisan program that provides mandates for all Americans. The filibuster gives a minority party with at least 41 votes in the Senate procedural rights to stop this drive for partisan dominance, even when the majority party has control of the presidency and both houses of Congress. This study has noted in the modern American legislative system the tension, even inconsistency, between the goals of bipartisan change, which is incremental, and fundamental change, which is partisan. The tension between political parties and the filibuster is the same tension, just in a broader context.

This tension between the goals of partisan parties and Senate minority rights is not new. Although the Founders swore off parties and tried to neutralize them in the Constitution, they quickly formed opposing coalitions. Washington, Adams, and Hamilton saw themselves as an elected government beset by people allied with France out to bring them down. Madison and Jefferson saw themselves as defending the fledgling republic from being transformed into a "Federalist-led, British backed monarchy."[2] By the 1820s, with the election of Andrew Jackson, the party beast was completely out of the cage; and, as noted earlier in the book, filibusters were under way in the Senate by the 1840s. Since then, the tension between these two mutations—party versus filibuster—has shaped much of American legislative history.

Again, this tension between partisan party objectives and Senate minority rights highlights the incompatibility of the critics' objectives. The filibuster, which gives us bipartisan legislation in the Senate, is the political counterweight to concerns over the negative consequences of more polarization and partisanship. Those concerned over the rising tide of polarization should welcome and support the filibuster. Those concerned over gridlock should support the abolition of the filibuster and wel-come the more partisan laws that will be the inevitable result.

For critics of the filibuster, there are two avenues. The first is that pursued by partisans of both sides, which is to elect enough senators to provide a "filibuster-proof" Sen-ate. Although the number needed is theoretically 60, my hunch is that 57 or more will be enough. There are al-ways several moderates who can be recruited on an is-sue-by-issue basis to help obtain the 60 votes needed for cloture—like the three Republican senators who sup-ported the economic stimulus package in early 2009. The key for the majority is not to openly insult the minority and have them harden into an implacable minority.

The other choice for those concerned over gridlock is eliminating the filibuster. Ironically, the most intellectu-ally rigorous proponent of this view is Sarah Binder, the foremost scholar of the filibuster. For Binder, "a rapidly changing political environment has rendered the Sen-ate's inherited procedures incapable of serving the needs of the modern Senate."[3] For her, the filibuster was an oversight in the Senate rules whose negative impact has grown beyond any initial value. In response to David Mayhew's conclusion that the American legislative process has proven a resilient all-weather political ma-chine, producing major legislation at a constant rate, she notes that about 50 percent of the issues she considers "salient" go unaddressed.[4]

It is worth noting that Binder's solution of abolishing or weakening the filibuster would inject more partisanship into the legislative process.[5] The big winners from abolishing the filibuster would be the president and the political parties, which would see their proposals sail through a majoritarian Senate. The American legislative machine would take on a more parliamentary cast.

The Nuclear Option

The most straightforward way to abolish the filibuster would be the "nuclear option." Popular discussion of this surfaced when Senate Majority Leader Bill Frist proposed this during the ongoing struggle over judicial nominations in the Senate in 2005. Judicial nominations have become among the most partisan events in Washington. Public discussion of the "nuclear option" certainly did not escape partisan slant. The present rule provides that attaining cloture on any debate over changing a Senate rule requires a two-thirds vote of the Senate. Thus, to change the 60-vote requirement under Rule 22, proponents would need 67 votes.

Starting in the 1960s, a way through this thicket was developed by liberal senators seeking to pass civil rights legislation. Working off nineteenth-century precedents, Democratic senators such as Walter Mondale (Minn.) and George McGovern (S.D.) developed what is referred to as the "constitutional" or "nuclear" option. When Senator Frist mentioned that he might use the "nuclear option" for the nominations of federal judges, including those of Supreme Court nominees, political commentators went into a frenzy. Although subjected to an inordinate level of high-flying rhetoric, this constitutional option has two elements. First, it invokes Article I, Section 5, of the Constitution, which provides that "each House may determine the rules of its proceedings." For proponents of the constitutional option, this means that the Senate would use a majority vote to bypass the requirement of a two-thirds vote to invoke cloture on changing the 60-vote requirement of Rule 22.[6]

The second step of this process is virtually incomprehensible because of the arcane terminology of Senate procedure. The key to successfully employing the "constitutional" option is that an aggressive majority leader and a compliant vice president must work together to get the decisive vote framed as a "tabling motion" and not a cloture motion. Tabling motions are not debatable and can be sustained by a 51-vote majority.

For our purposes, two points are in order. The first is that although available, the "constitutional option" has never had a majority of senators in support of it. In 1888, then–Senate majority leader Nelson Aldrich of Rhode Island failed by one vote on the Force Bill to pass the "constitutional option."[7]

The second point returns us to Binder's position. The constitutional option is simply a procedural path to abolishing the filibuster. (Although Senator Frist limited his proposal to judicial nominations, the constitutional option could be applied to legislation.) If adopted, the partisans and the president are the winners. The question is why senators of the majority party are unwilling to support the constitutional option. The reason is that

they are rational. The filibuster, along with its procedural cousin the "hold," maximizes the power of individual senators. It gives them the power to offer amendments and to hold up legislation, even if it is legislation
sponsored by their own party. In addition, senators are
usually seeking careers that span several presidents.
Since 1980, there have been six changes of party control in the United States Senate. The question is, how
should an individual senator react to these changes?
Should she be willing to give up her rights when in the
minority for greater legislative success when in the majority? Game theory provides us with a ready answer.
The min-max doctrine of game theory tells us that a rational decisionmaker makes the best of her worst case
prospects.[8] For a senator, the worst case is being a member of the minority party in the Senate. Thus, a rational
senator would seek to maximize her leverage when she
is in the minority. This means support for her right to filibuster and opposition to the constitutional option. This
calculation of individual senators is unlikely to change
in the future.

The American Legislative Machine

Americans have consciously used competition for a variety of purposes. For our material well-being, we rely
on competitive markets. In the pursuit of justice, we
have employed an adversarial judicial system. To foster
a healthy democracy and provide us policy choices for
collective action, we have employed two political parties

for more than 180 years. The number two has turned out to be an ideal number. The two parties can be used by the electorate to check each other, but they have not broken into smaller factions and spawned a confusing swirl of splinter groups unable to serve the underlying consensus for democracy that is at the heart of the American experience.

Yet these two political parties come with a risk. The goal of each party is to storm the barriers embedded in the Constitution that protect us from the propensity of ambitious politicians to achieve personal glory through excessive and intrusive lawmaking. Most of all, the Constitution is a document on human psychology that provides us with a basis for cooperation and safeguards us against the dark side of human nature. Scholars have only begun to probe the interaction of our basic humanity and the democratic process. And as scholars learn more about the shortcomings of the human mind —particularly its jury-rigged structure, its tendency to self-righteousness, and its extreme self-confidence when making rapid-fire judgments based on limited information—I am confident that we will only increase our appreciation of the need for caution in our political processes.

For more than 150 years, the constitutional barriers have been augmented by the existence of a package of minority rights in the Senate, based on the filibuster. Thus, while we have used the parties to check each other, we have used the filibuster to check the dominant party of the moment. Protecting and enhancing the values, prosperity, and security of 300 million Americans is far too complex and important a task for any political party that can only lurch in two-year increments from election to election. Though we accord the winner power and prestige, we force the winners to negotiate with their opponents before they can pass binding rules that affect our lives, families, and futures. This should be a slow, grinding process. Good, sound ideas are rare, and they are especially rare in the long, rambling lists that pass for party platforms.

Of equal risk to the electorate are the interest groups cozily nestled under the party banners. Their rallying cry of serving the public interest is a smokescreen for the particular gains they hope to achieve through the legislative process. While over a 140 million Americans go to work, help their families, and pay taxes, skilled practitioners of the legislative arts seek individual advantage for themselves and their clients, often at the public's expense and certainly with the public's tax dollars. This seeking of private gain through the legislative process is an inherent risk in the legislative process of every democracy. In America, we have enshrined this in the First Amendment's right of the people "to petition the government for a redress of grievances." Checking these partisan groups through the exercise of minority rights in the Senate is a valuable piece of our democracy's defensive system against this phenomenon.[9]

No virtue is unalloyed. In politics, there is less truth and right and wrong at stake than its partisans will admit. Politics is the arena of trade-offs, the best available option, and assessing consequences. And if done with some intellectual honesty, it can consist of admitting undesirable, unintended consequences. The filibuster is not an unalloyed good. It can slow the consideration of legislation. Its use has led to an atrophying of the authorization and appropriations processes within the Senate and the entire Congress. Certainly, the nominees of the judicial and executive branches have been harshly and sometimes unfairly treated. Ultimately, solving or alleviating these undesirable consequences of Senate minority rights falls back on the senators themselves. As a shared institution between the parties, its inner workings and performance are entrusted to them. And if the electorate is dissatisfied, it retains the right to remove them and bring in fresh blood.

Certainly, over the next decade, the American legislative process will be severely tested. Quietly embedded in President Barack Obama's news conference on February 8, 2009, on the eve of victory for his economic stimulus legislation, was the shape of the future legislative Armageddon that is inexorably forming on the horizon. The president noted that the federal deficits for 2009 and 2010 "pale in comparison to what we're going to be seeing 10 or 15 or 20 years down the road."[10]

Along the way, in the short discussion on entitlements in chapter 5, I noted that the federal government has promised $40 to $50 trillion more in benefits than is presently available in revenues. Moreover, I noted that the strongest set of emotional defense mechanisms available to the human species has been triggered to fight for the continuation of these existing benefits. In wading into this fiscal and emotional thicket, President Obama and his successors are limited to four unwelcome policy options: increased taxes, reduced benefits, increased deficit spending, or some combination of these three.

This study has shown that in addressing this emerging issue of entitlement reform, the American legislative system has at its disposal two gears. One is the incremental bipartisan gear that provides for slow and heavily contested progress, but has a long history of success in building the great American consensus so eloquently described by Hilley.[11] The other gear is the rapid, sweeping partisan change found in the reconciliation process. In this case, one political party with unified control of the federal government can impose its preferred solution without the hard slog of negotiating with a Senate minority possessing the full arsenal of the Minority Tool Kit. Although such a sweeping solution could be quickly enacted, it runs the risk that it could be unstable. The partisanship inherent in the reconciliation process leaves any of its enactments subject to a successful legislative counterattack if there is major electoral change and the other party gains full control of the federal government. Thus, the tax cuts of the Ronald Reagan era in the 1980s triggered President Bill Clinton's reconciliation effort in 1993 that repealed some of the Reagan cuts, which in turn spawned the use of reconciliation by George W. Bush's administration to again cut taxes in 2001 and 2003.

For practitioners of the legislative process who make a living muddling through these apparently unsolvable conundrums, it is always worth remembering Woody Allen's wry analysis: "More than any time in history, mankind faces a crossroads. One path leads to despair and hopelessness, the other to total extinction. Let us pray we have the wisdom to choose correctly."

What the American legislative system does not provide is the cure-all of a bipartisan tool for rapid structural change. But this is the vain hope of theory, not reality. As always, we should end with Madison: "If men were angels, no government would be necessary."[12]

 # Notes

Introduction

1. Michel de Montaigne, quoted by Geoffrey Parker, *Europe in Crisis, 1598–1648*, 5th ed. (London: Fontana, 1988), 115. This quotation is both self-serving and on point.

2. See James McGregor Burns, *The Deadlock of Democracy: Four-Party Politics in America* (New York: Prentice Hall, 1963); Robert Bendiner, *Obstacle Course on Capitol Hill* (New York: McGraw-Hill, 1964); Roger H. Davidson, David M. Kovenock, and Michael K. O'Leary, *Congress in Crisis: Politics and Congressional Reform* (Belmont, Calif.: Wadsworth, 1966); and Joseph S. Clark, *Congress: The Sapless Branch* (New York: Harper & Row, 1964).

3. Burns, *Deadlock of Democracy*, 1.

4. Ibid., 323–25. Jefferson's view approaches that of a majoritarian parliamentary system: "Be this as it may, in every free and deliberating society, there must, from the nature of man, be opposite parties, and violent dissensions and discords; and one of these, for the most part, must prevail over the other for a longer or shorter time. Perhaps this party division is necessary to induce each to watch and relate to the people the proceedings of the other." Merrill Peterson, *Thomas Jefferson and the New Nation* (New York: Oxford University Press, 1975), 610.

5. See Thomas E. Mann and Norman J. Ornstein, *The Broken Branch: How Congress Is Failing America and How to Get It Back on Track* (New York: Oxford University Press, 2006); Ronald Brownstein, *The Second Civil War: How Extreme Partisanship Has Paralyzed Washington and Polarized America* (New York: Penguin, 2007); Barbara Sinclair, *Party Wars: Polarization and the Politics of National Policy Making* (Norman: University of Oklahoma Press, 2006); Nolan McCarty et al., *Polarized America: The Dance of Ideology and Unequal Riches* (Cambridge, Mass.: MIT

Press, 2006); Sarah Binder, *Stalemate: Causes and Consequences of Legislative Gridlock* (Washington, D.C.: Brookings Institution Press, 2003); and Juliet Eilperin, *Fight Club Politics: How Partisanship Is Poisoning the House of Representatives* (Stanford, Calif.: Hoover Institution Press, 2006). *Party Wars* by Barbara Sinclair and *Stalemate* by Sarah Binder are included here for their titles rather than content. They are nuanced and balanced accounts of the modern legislative process.

6. The use of these titles creates an obvious intellectual "straw man." The "party accountability" view of the 1950 American Political Science Association report was critiqued by Pendleton Herring and others. In his *Politics of Democracy* (New York: W. W. Norton, 1965), Herring emphasizes the fluid nature of the parties and their important role in reaching negotiated settlements on issues of national importance. On the view that today's legislative process is dysfunctional and stymied by partisan gridlock, the Brookings Institution has produced two volumes of academic essays titled *Red and Blue Nation* that provide critics with a forum; see *Red and Blue Nation: Characteristics and Causes of America's Polarized Politics*, ed. David W. Brady and Pietro S. Nivola (Washington, D.C., and Stanford, Calif.: Brookings Institution Press and Hoover Institution Press), vol. 1, 2006; and vol. 2, 2008. Regardless of the existence of academic dissent on particulars, the "straw man" has the value of representing a highly influential perspective within the academic community and the overwhelming view among journalists and the American public.

7. E. J. Dionne, *Washington Post*, November 5, 2008.

8. David Broder, *Washington Post*, November 6, 2008.

9. *New York Times*, February 12, 2009; and *Washington Post*, January 28, 2009.

10. See Donald Wolfensberger, *Congress and the People: Deliberative Democracy on Trial* (Baltimore: Johns Hopkins University Press, 2000); and John Hilley, *The Challenge of Legislation: Bipartisanship in a Partisan World* (Washington, D.C.: Brookings Institution Press, 2008).

11. The other superb treatment of the modern legislative process is Bob Woodward's *The Agenda*. This is less analytic than Hilley's work, but it accurately captures the punch and gouge of the early Clinton legislative efforts in 1993. Moreover, its observation that "politics is about contested ground" offers a pithy and accurate description of the legislative process worth remembering. Bob Woodward, *The Agenda: Inside the Clinton White House* (New York: Simon & Schuster, 1994).

12. Hilley, *Challenge of Legislation*, 228.

13. Ibid., 229.

14. Ibid., 230.

15. As the Supreme Court noted in the 1973 Nixon case, opposing sides provide "that concrete adverseness which sharpens the presentation of issues upon which the court so largely depends for illumination of difficult constitutional questions." *U.S. v. Nixon,* 418 U.S. 683, 1974.

16. In 1999, I put together a policy report for my seminar at the College of William and Mary titled *The Art of Legislation: A Practitioner's Guide.* Revised and streamlined portions of that report are found woven throughout this study.

17. Although the degree of polarization is important to the "hyperpartisans," it is not critical to this study. Keith Krehbiel of Stanford has noted that polarization measures may overstate the degree of polarization by up to 42 percent because unanimous (and sometimes near-unanimous) roll call votes are dropped from the data sets. See Keith Krehbiel, "Comments," in *Red and Blue Nation,* ed. Brady and Nivola, vol. 2, 99. A recent paper by Michael Lynch of the University of Kansas and Anthony Madonna at Washington University in Saint Louis also notes that voting data may be skewed by ignoring voice votes. Because these voice votes have been treated differently by Congress over the years, it may cause consistency problems when comparing voting patterns over time. See Michael Lynch and Anthony Madonna, "Viva Voce: Implications from the Disappearing Voice Vote, 1807–1990," paper presented at the Midwest Political Science Association meeting, Chicago, March 2008. I plan to avoid these data knife fights at all costs.

18. Jerome H. Barkow, Leda Cosmides, and John Tooby, *The Adapted Mind: Evolutionary Psychology and the Generation of Culture* (New York: Oxford University Press, 1992), 79.

19. This area of research is gaining momentum and widely reported in the press. In 2005, Hibbing published a study relating genes and political preferences in a study in the *American Political Science Review* that was reported in the *New York Times* on June 21, 2005. Studies by the biologist David Sloan Wilson (reported in the February 23, 2008, *Economist*) and psychologist Johnathan Haidt (reported in the October 18, 2007, *New York Times*) have reached similar conclusions. In particular, Wilson and Haidt have found that those genetically predisposed to be liberals are more individualistic, while conservatives are more group oriented. Of interest to students of legislative gridlock, both Wilson and Haidt agree that conservatives and liberals see issues in moral terms declaring their view "right" and those of their political

opponents as "immoral." Interestingly, these differences have been noted before by skilled observers. Before the scientists got involved, in the 1957 book *The Citadel,* which made popular the notion of the Senate as a "club," the author, William White, noted differences between Republican and Democratic senators. Republicans were more cohesive and single-minded. In contrast, Democrats were better improvisers, more articulate, and better political "operators." William White, *The Citadel: The Story of the U.S. Senate* (New York: Harper Brothers, 1957), 199–209. For a recent summary of the scientific progress in this field, see James Fowler and Darren Schreiber, "Biology, Politics, and the Emerging Science of Human Nature," *Science,* November 7, 2008, 912–14.

20. See Marc Hauser, *Moral Minds: How Nature Designed Our Universal Sense of Right and Wrong* (New York: HarperCollins, 2006). For a general overview of this, see the recent article "The Roots of Morality," *Science,* May 9, 2008, 734.

21. Robert Wright, *The Moral Animal: Why We Are, the Way We Are—The New Science of Evolutionary Psychology* (New York: Pantheon, 1994), 12. Peter Singer, the controversial liberal Princeton philosophy professor, has urged the left to adopt "an approach to human behavior based firmly on a modern understanding of human nature." Peter Singer, *Ethical Life* (New York: HarperCollins, 2001), 273. Little of this is new. Aristotle captured the major elements of this new science of human nature almost 2,500 years ago when he noted: "It is true that in the give and take of mutual services this kind of justice—reciprocity of treatment—forms the bond between the parts of the process. . . . It is just the feeling that, as one does, so one will be done by, that keeps a political association in being." Aristotle, *The Nicomachean Ethics* (Baltimore: Penguin, 1958), 151.

22. Sinclair, *Party Wars,* 232.

23. Given the larger Senate Democratic majority resulting from the 2008 election, the Senate Democratic leadership will need only de minimis bipartisan participation from Senate Republicans to pass legislation.

24. Brownstein, *Second Civil War,* 127. It is also worth noting that theme of bringing us together for fundamental change started with Nixon and his slogan "Bring Us Together"; *Washington Post,* January 7, 2008.

25. Michel de Montaigne, *The Complete Works: Of Custom,* Everyman Library (New York: Alfred A. Knopf, 2003), 259.

Chapter 1

1. Charles O. Jones, quoted by Keith Krehbiel, *Pivotal Politics: A Theory of U.S. Lawmaking* (Chicago: University of Chicago Press, 1998), 20.

2. Barbara Sinclair, "Spoiling the Sausages? How a Polarized Congress Deliberates and Legislates," in *Red and Blue Nation: Characteristics and Causes of America's Polarized Politics,* vol. 2, ed. David W. Brady and Pietro S. Nivola (Washington, D.C., and Stanford, Calif.: Brookings Institution Press and Hoover Institution Press, 2008), 70.

3. Quoted by Mark Peterson, *Legislating Together: The White House and Capitol Hill from Eisenhower to Reagan* (Cambridge, Mass.: Harvard University Press, 1990), 4. Corwin's statement related to foreign policy, but over the years it has been often quoted with respect to all policymaking under the Constitution.

4. Addicts of the legislative process can read Tom Reid, *Congressional Odyssey: The Saga of a Senate Bill* (San Francisco: W. H. Freeman, 1980), which charts the many twists and turns of this bill.

5. Barbara Sinclair, *Unorthodox Lawmaking: New Legislative Processes in the U.S. Congress* (Washington, D.C.: CQ Press, 2000), 224.

6. Paul Bedard, "Washington Whispers," *US News & World Report* online, www.usnews.com, June 25, 2007.

7. In 1999, I put this little triangle in the manual for my course at William and Mary. During the course of doing background reading for this book, I have come upon a whole academic theory of legislation known as Pivot Theory. Although Pivot Theory starts with the same observations that I learned from experience—the importance of the veto and filibuster—it does not place the same emphasis as I do on the House Rules Committee. There is a vast academic literature for and against the Pivot Theory. Because I have only one life to live, I am not taking sides on the details other than to state that with the triangle, I start at the same place as the proponents of Pivot Theory. Where the proponents and their critics end up, I leave to academic battles still under way.

Chapter 2

1. Like any weapon in an arsenal, a veto does not have to be used to be effective. Knowledge of its existence alters the strategy of other participants. Political theorists refer to this as the "rule of anticipated

reactions." This rule also applies to the filibuster that will be discussed below.

2. *New York Times,* April 2, 1995. Guilt assuaged, the problem is now that most students have little idea of the authoritarian extremes of the old Soviet Union.

3. Ronald Brownstein, *The Second Civil War: How Extreme Partisanship Has Paralyzed Washington and Polarized America* (New York: Penguin, 2007), 79.

4. *New York Times,* December 27, 2006.

5. *Washington Post,* February 18, 2007. For in-depth examples, see Don Wolfensberger's columns in the March 31, 2008, and the April 14, 2008, issues of *Roll Call.*

6. Donald Wolfensberger, *Congress and the People: Deliberative Democracy on Trial* (Baltimore: Johns Hopkins University Press, 2000), 46.

7. Sarah Binder, *Minority Rights, Minority Rule: Partisanship and the Development of Congress* (Cambridge: Cambridge University Press, 1997), 132. This telescoped discussion of the accretion of power in the House Rules Committee shortchanges the period from 1937 to 1970. In 1937, President Franklin Delano Roosevelt tried to expand or "pack" the Supreme Court by increasing its membership. This triggered a violent reaction from Southern Democrats and Republicans. After 1937, substantial power was vested in the committee chairmen in the House, most of whom were from the South. It was against this phalanx of Southern chairmen that the House Democratic leadership began its efforts in the 1970s to reassert and expand the power of the Rules Committee.

8. Ibid., 154.

9. Ibid., 163.

10. Ibid., 154–55.

11. There can be solid reasons for restrictive rules. In 1995, when the Republicans considered an open rule, the Democrats responded by submitting approximately 600 amendments. The tale of the House Rules Committee is not just one of minorities being victimized by the majority. It is also a tale of minority obstruction.

12. Even this minority right has been subject to erosion. For the procedural particulars, see Donald Wolfsensberger's April 9, 2008, *Roll Call* column and a *Washington Post* editorial of January 12, 2009. Interestingly, as Wolfensberger notes elsewhere, such "manipulation" of the rules previously has been seen by historians, political scientists, and activist partisans as a "sign of strong party leadership." Wolfensberger, *Congress and the People,* 274.

13. Brownstein, *Second Civil War,* 338.

14. David Linden, *The Accidental Mind: How Brain Evolution Has Given Us Love, Memory, Dreams, and God* (Cambridge, Mass.: Harvard University Press, 2007), 11–12.

15. Because we will return these shortcomings of human nature, the following description of the human brain is a refreshing antidote to self-delusion and self-importance to which we all fall prey: "The brain is not elegantly designed by any means: it is a cobbled together mess. . . . More important, the quirky inefficient and bizarre plan of the brain and its constituent parts is fundamental to our human experience. The particular texture of our feelings, perceptions, and actions is derived, in large part, from the fact that the brain is not an optimized generic problem-solving machine, but rather a weird agglomeration of ad hoc solutions that have accumulated throughout millions of years of evolutionary history." Linden, *Accidental Mind,* 3. To cap it off, our brains are "unreliable and slow." "Incredibly, with few exceptions, the neurons and glial cells in a worm are not substantially different from those in our own brains." Ibid., 29. In fact, another student of the human brain notes that the channel proteins still used in the human brain first showed up in bacteria. Jean-Pierre Changeux, *The Physiology of Truth: Neuroscience and Human Knowledge* (Cambridge, Mass.: Harvard University Press, 2004),18.

16. Barbara Sinclair, *Party Wars: Polarization and the Politics of National Policy Making* (Norman: University of Oklahoma Press, 2006), xv.

17. E.g., see Thomas E. Mann and Norman J. Ornstein, *The Broken Branch: How Congress Is Failing America and How to Get It Back on Track* (New York: Oxford University Press, 2006), 29.

18. Robert Remini, *The House: The History of the U.S. House of Representatives* (New York: HarperCollins, 2006), 155.

19. Keith Krehbiel, *Pivotal Politics: A Theory of U.S. Lawmaking* (Chicago: University of Chicago Press, 1998), xiii.

20. See Steven Pinker, "The Moral Instinct," *New York Times Magazine,* January 13, 2008; and Robert Hinde, *Bending the Rules: Morality in the Modern World—From Relationships to Politics and War* (Oxford: Oxford University Press, 2007), 24.

21. Robert Wright, *The Moral Animal: Why We Are, the Way We Are—The New Science of Evolutionary Psychology* (New York: Pantheon, 1994), 280. Harvey Mansfield of Harvard has an edgier view, which is that "people go into politics to pick a fight, not to avoid one." See Harvey Mansfield, "How to Understand Politics: What the Humani-

ties Can Say to Science," 2007 Jefferson Lecture in the Humanities, National Endowment for the Arts (www.neh.gov/whoweare/mansfield/HMlecture.html), 5.

22. Steven Pinker, *How the Mind Works* (New York: W. W. Norton, 1997), 513–14. It is well established that just because something is "natural" or part of human nature does not make it right. But as Jerome Barkow and his colleagues correctly note, for those "genuinely concerned" about improving man's lot, a knowledge of human nature is a prerequisite for "possible successful interventions to bring about humane outcomes. Moreover, a program of social melioration carried on in ignorance of human complex design is something like letting a blindfolded individual loose in an operating room with a scalpel—there is likely to be more blood than healing." Jerome H. Barkow, Leda Cosmides, and John Tooby, *The Adapted Mind: Evolutionary Psychology and the Generation of Culture* (New York: Oxford University Press, 1992), 40.

23. Michael S. Gazzaniga, *Human: The Science behind What Makes Us Unique* (New York: HarperCollins, 2008), 74.

24. See *Science,* April 29, 2006, 15. Also see Marc Hauser, *Moral Minds: How Nature Designed Our Universal Sense of Right and Wrong* (New York: HarperCollins, 2006), 103, 272. In the October 15, 2005, *Economist,* 82, the game theorist Robert Aumann points out the value of "vengeful retaliation." He notes that one player will collaborate with another only because he knows if he is cheated today, he can punish the cheat tomorrow.

25. Robert Axelrod, *The Evolution of Cooperation* (New York: Basic Books, 1984), 73–87.

26. As far as I can tell, both parties in the House support the winner-take-all system. Both Democratic and Republican House members and staff are quite vocal that the Senate is an unmanageable legislative "swamp." Henry Waxman noted that if the House majority were united, the minority was "irrelevant." This is a sentiment to which Newt Gingrich, Dennis Hastert, and Nancy Pelosi would all say "amen."

27. Representative Cole, who was a professor of political science before becoming a member of Congress, also makes the point that it is the closeness of the vote margins between the parties in the House, and not polarization, that lead to the intensity of House politics. Regardless, if control of either the House or Senate at election time depends on the fate of only several seats, the fighting will be fierce, on and off the floor.

Chapter 3

1. Quoted by Susan Dunn, *Sister Revolutions: French Lightning, American Light* (New York: Faber, 1999), 69.

2. Sarah Binder, the filibuster's foremost student, has characterized it as an example of "unintended consequences." Sarah Binder, *Stalemate: Causes and Consequences of Legislative Gridlock* (Washington, D.C.: Brookings Institution Press, 2003), 13.

3. Ibid., 13.

4. Gregory Wawro and Eric Schikler, *Filibuster: Obstruction and Lawmaking in the U.S. Senate* (Princeton, N.J.: Princeton University Press, 2006), 14.

5. Ibid., 74.

6. Senator Thomas Hart Benton, 1897, quoted by Binder, *Stalemate,* 181.

7. Ibid., 167.

8. Sarah Binder and Steven Smith, *Politics or Principle? Filibustering in the United States Senate* (Washington, D.C.: Brookings Institution Press, 1997), 66.

9. Ibid., 60.

10. Franklin L. Burdette, *Filibustering in the Senate* (Princeton, N.J.: Princeton University Press, 1940), quoted by Binder and Smith *Politics or Principle?* 87.

11. See Wawro and Schickler, *Filibuster,* 212.

12. This is the practical effect. Technically, the bill remains the pending business and can be the subject of further discussion. There can be multiple cloture votes on the same bill, and sometimes the majority will wear the minority down or a negotiated settlement will end the dispute and allow the bill to move forward.

13. In the House, the Rules Committee can provide a waiver making a nongermane amendment in order. In the Senate, there are germaneness requirements on appropriations bills.

14. There is a dynamic interplay between the majority and minority in the Senate. E.g., there are cases where the minority does not want to kill an entire bill but wants to use its leverage to resist certain amendments of the majority. In such cases, a unanimous consent request is granted where the minority allows for the adoption of cloture, but certain amendments must gain a 60-vote majority to be accepted. Such "targeted filibusters" have been increasing over the past two years.

15. There is a procedural option known as "filing the amendment tree," which is used by the majority leader to fill all possible amendment slots, thus limiting any member from offering an amendment. This tactic has been increasingly used over the past several years. The downside of the tactic is that its mere use may trigger a retaliatory filibuster by the minority.

16. The FSC/ETI is the Foreign Sales Corporation and Extraterritorial Income Act.

17. For a good discussion of "holds," see Barbara Sinclair, *Party Wars: Polarization and the Politics of National Policy Making* (Norman: University of Oklahoma Press, 2006), 205–11.

18. For years, I have referred to the Senate floor as the swamp, but "iceberg" is more accurate. See ibid., 210.

Chapter 4

1. The 1974 Budget Act was a Democratic response to the impoundment of appropriated water pollution control funds by President Richard Nixon. The first time reconciliation was used was in 1980 by Senator Edmund Muskie (D-Maine). He used it for its original purpose, described in the following paragraph in the text, which was at the end of the fiscal year to balance the budget books.

2. Surprisingly, as late as 2006, McCarty et al referred to reconciliation as a "gimmick." Nolan McCarty et al., *Polarized America: The Dance of Ideology and Unequal Riches* (Cambridge, Mass.: MIT Press, 2006), 179. This comment misses the strategic value and history of reconciliation.

3. Political mutations are common in history. Democracy itself could be characterized as a mutation. In ancient Athens, the Alcueonid clan was being pushed from power. In a bold, spontaneous stroke to maintain power, the clan's leader, Cleisthenes, proposed from the floor of a public meeting to rewrite the constitution so that sovereign power resided with adult male citizens. Robin Fox, *The Classical World: An Epic History from Homer to Hadrian* (New York: Basic Books, 2006), 87.

4. These lists only include those items discussed in this study and are not complete lists of all the offensive and defensive legislative tools available to both parties. One obvious omission is the use of conferences by the majority as an offensive tool. In my 1999 manual, I examine conferences at some length. They are a subtle, and often con-

tentious, negotiating forum. However, because minorities can filibuster conference reports if they so choose, these nuances do not affect the overall thread of the argument here on the central role of filibusters.

5. There are some important examples of bipartisan reconciliation bills. In 1997, President Bill Clinton, a Democrat, and Newt Gingrich and Trent Lott, the Republican leaders of the House and Senate, respectively, joined forces to pass a balanced budget reconciliation bill. But the rarity of this bipartisan effort only highlights the fundamentally partisan nature of most reconciliation legislation.

Chapter 5

1. The notion that private parties enter the legislative forum to achieve narrow interests can be troubling to some, including myself. But some needed perspective is provided by G. R. Elton in his study of the English Parliament from 1559 to 1581, where he raises the issue of whether the elected representatives are even in charge: "Prolonged involvement with Parliament has in the end convinced me that the customary concentration on it as the center of public affairs, however traditional it may be, is entirely misleading. I now wonder whether the institution . . . ever really mattered all that much in the politics of the nation, except perhaps as a stage sometimes used by the real contenders over government and policy. But it is a highly sophisticated instrument for the making of law and a means available to all sorts of Englishmen in the pursuit of their ends. It gathered in the particles of the nation and in turn threw light upon their concerns." G. R. Elton, *The Parliament of England: 1559–1581* (Cambridge: Cambridge University Press, 1989), ix.

2. Completing this legislative taxonomy would require that after identifying "landmark" and "important" bills, the remainder of the other bills passed each Congress would be divided between "routine" and "ceremonial." Paul Light, a professor at New York University, in a November 11, 2008, *Washington Post* article that discussed the prospects for President Barack Obama's first-year legislation, used a comparable three-part classification of "supersize," "major," and "first-year" legislation.

3. Taxes and entitlements have also been included in reconciliation bills over the years. This is a decision that is determined by the budget resolution in any given year.

4. The third major entitlement, Medicaid, is under the Finance Committee in the Senate but under the Energy and Commerce Committee in the House.

5. Louis Fisher, *Constitutional Conflict between Congress and the President,* 3rd ed. (Lawrence: University Press of Kansas, 1991), 193. Entitlements do have some differences from other authorizations. The most important of these is that they are not subject to the normal constraints of the annual appropriations process. Debt-limit legislation could also be included here. But it has a complicated history, and a thorough discussion would take us far afield.

6. Samuel Bowles, *Microeconomics* (Princeton, N.J.: Princeton University Press, 2004), 104. Robert Frank, *Passion within Reason* (New York: W. W. Norton, 1988), 77–80.

7. In the winter of 1995–96, the Republicans "mugged" the "payroll clerk" and shut down the federal government several times in a budget struggle with President Clinton, who emerged as the clear political winner in this contest.

8. CRs, omnis, and supps can be filibustered, but this is usually done to trigger negotiations, not to kill the underlying appropriations.

9. The House had a longer list of priorities, which it could more easily process.

10. Andrea Campbell, "Comments," in *Red and Blue Nation: Characteristics and Causes of America's Polarized Politics,* vol. 2, ed. David W. Brady and Pietro S. Nivola (Washington, D.C., and Stanford, Calif.: Brookings Institution Press and Hoover Institution Press, 2008), 221.

11. This notion is taken from Mark Peterson's description of the "constrained" conflict between presidents and Congress and applied here to the relations between the Senate majority and minority. Mark Peterson, *Legislating Together: The White House and Capitol Hill from Eisenhower to Reagan* (Cambridge, Mass.: Harvard University Press, 1990), 78.

Chapter 6

1. David W. Brady and Hahrie C. Han, "Polarization Then and Now: A Historical Perspective," in *Red and Blue Nation: Characteristics and Causes of America's Polarized Politics,* vol. 1, ed. David W. Brady and Pietro S. Nivola (Washington, D.C., and Stanford, Calif.: Brookings Institution Press and Hoover Institution Press, 2006), 131.

2. Some scholars have been dismissive of today's cries of partisanship. Writing in 2000, Gordon Wood, perhaps our foremost historian

of early America, noted: "In the last decade of the early eighteenth century Americans were more fiercely divided than they would be until the time of the Civil War. Compared to the frenzied and divisive politics in the era of the Founding Fathers, our own turn of the century political scene seems remarkable stable, staid, and respectable"; Gordon S. Wood, "An Affair of Honor," *New York Review of Books,* April 13, 2000, 67. The well-regarded Civil War historian James McPherson has echoed Wood's words: "During the 1850's when representatives came armed to the floor of Congress, fistfights between Northerners and Southerners broke out in the House and a South Carolina congressman clubbed a Massachusetts senator almost to death with a heavy cane on the floor of the Senate as the nation drifted toward civil war. The partisanship and political polarization in Washington during recent years has been child's play compared with those events a century and a half ago"; *New York Review of Books,* December 16, 2004, 70. Because it is impossible to pile on too much with respect to this point, let me conclude this footnote with the following summation from Galston and Nivola: "For all the hype about the ruptures and partisan rancor in contemporary American society, the strife pales in comparison with much of the nation's past." William A. Galston and Pietro S. Nivola, "Introduction," in *Red and Blue Nation,* vol. 1, ed. Brady and Nivola, 7.

3. Doris Kearns Goodwin, quoted by David Mayhew, *Divided We Govern: Policy Control, Lawmaking, and Investigations, 1946–1990,* 2nd ed. (New Haven, Conn.: Yale University Press, 2005), 181.

4. Alexis de Tocqueville, quoted in ibid., 183. Don Wolfensberger, in his public presentations, has noted that if you are looking for perfection in the legislative process, "you are on the wrong planet."

5. Mayhew's work has generated its own cottage industry of responses. Much of the critique is along the lines of that noted in the discussion of Sarah Binder's work under the "nuclear" option in chapter 7—namely, that whereas Mayhew shows that the American legislative process manages to produce a steady flow of "important" legislation regardless of whether government is divided or united, the rate of output, because of the filibuster, is not adequate to meet the challenges of the modern world.

6. Mayhew, *Divided We Govern,* 82–83.

7. Ibid., 218.

8. Galston and Nivola, "Introduction," 29. Binder also notes that issues of "salience" have a higher likelihood of passage. Sarah Binder, *Stalemate: Causes and Consequences of Legislative Gridlock* (Washington,

D.C.: Brookings Institution Press, 2003), 96. Barbara Sinclair has a more cautious appraisal: "True gridlock would be a serious problem, but that is not a correct description of the current state of affairs." Barbara Sinclair, *Party Wars: Polarization and the Politics of National Policy Making* (Norman: University of Oklahoma Press, 2006), 356. Using a different set of assumptions, Sinclair notes that the "survival rate" of "major bills" has declined from 82 percent in the 1960s and 1970s to 67 percent from the late 1970s to the early 2000s. As a practitioner, it is tough to declare a two-thirds passage rate a crisis in itself. The question is which ones have failed and how do you make anything approaching an objective analysis of the importance of this decline. Each side of the political aisle will either cheer or mourn the defeat of particular bills among the losing one-third or the winning two-thirds.

9. Binder, *Stalemate*, 60. Binder's quotation is in response to the first edition of Mayhew's work, which focused on the period 1945–90. The second edition took the analysis through 2002.

10. See Binder's analysis; Binder, *Stalemate*, 94, 97. Also, this is the gist of the exchange between Cole and Stark cited in chapter 2.

11. Binder and Sinclair both have conducted quantitative analyses to confirm this. Binder, *Stalemate*, 97–98; Sinclair, *Party Wars*, 227.

12. A good example of the Mayhew winning ugly school of thought is a June 21, 2008, *New York Times* article, which notes that "after months of sniping and stalemate, a hyper-partisan Congress is experiencing a sudden burst of harmony and productivity." In addition to passing terror surveillance legislation, "swift deals" were reached on war spending, extension of unemployment benefits and a new college program for veterans. The article continues: "Has a new day dawned on Capitol Hill? Perhaps, but it is Election Day members are really worried about." Mayhew would have written the same piece without the hype.

13. Thus, after the 9/11 attacks, the Democratic Senate minority worked closely with President George W. Bush and the Republican congressional majority to respond with new national security legislation.

14. Thomas Schelling of Harvard, one of the foremost game theorists, notes that some see conflict as a "pathological" condition requiring treatment, whereas others see conflict as inherent in the human condition. He goes on to state that "most conflict situations are inherently bargaining situations." Thomas Schelling, *The Strategy of Conflict* (Cambridge, Mass.: Harvard University Press, 1980), 5. With respect to the legislative process, the second assumption is accurate.

15. Ronald Brownstein, *The Second Civil War: How Extreme Partisanship Has Paralyzed Washington and Polarized America* (New York: Penguin, 2007), 58. Also sharing elements of this "Golden Age" view are Nolan McCarty et al., *Polarized America: The Dance of Ideology and Unequal Riches* (Cambridge, Mass.: MIT Press, 2006); and Thomas E. Mann and Norman J. Ornstein, *The Broken Branch: How Congress Is Failing America and How to Get It Back on Track* (New York: Oxford University Press, 2006).

16. Galston and Nivola, "Introduction," 3.

17. James McGregor Burns, *The Deadlock of Democracy: Four-Party Politics in America* (New York: Prentice Hall, 1963); Robert A. Caro, *Master of the Senate: The Years of Lyndon Johnson* (New York: Vintage, 2003), 385.

18. William White, *The Citadel: The Story of the U.S. Senate* (New York: Harper Brothers, 1957), 68.

19. Caro, *Master of the Senate*, 767.

20. These partisan elements of the debate are not usually mentioned in polite company. Brownstein alludes to it in *Civil War.* Also, Wolfensberger calls Ornstein and Mann to account in "A House Divided," his review of their *Broken Branch*, in the *Wilson Quarterly*, July 24, 2008, www.wilsoncenter.org/index.cfm?fuseaction=wq.essay&essay_id=204033. Joel Aberbach of the University of California, Los Angeles, also notes an element "of 'bad sport' sentiment at work, reflecting discontent with the outcome of recent elections." Joel Aberbach, "Comments," in *Red and Blue Nation: Characteristics and Causes of America's Polarized Politics*, vol. 2, ed. David W. Brady and Pietro S. Nivola (Washington, D.C., and Stanford, Calif.: Brookings Institution Press and Hoover Institution Press, 2008), 289.

21. For a more scholarly but less literary account, see Edward Carmines and James Stimson, *Race and the Transformation of American Politics* (Princeton, N.J.: Princeton University Press, 1989).

22. Brownstein, *Second Civil War*, 217.

23. Ibid., 371.

24. Ibid., 7.

25. The actual quotation is the "past often gets polished in our memories." Jason Zweig, *Your Money and Your Brain* (New York: Simon & Schuster, 2007), 23.

26. Elmer Eric Schattschneider, quoted favorably by Charles Stewart III, "Congress and the Constitutional System," in *Institutions of Democracy: The Legislative Branch*, ed. Paul Quick and Sarah Binder (New York: Oxford University Press, 2005), 30.

27. Charles Darwin, quoted by Samuel Bowles, *Microeconomics* (Princeton, N.J.: Princeton University Press, 2004), 445.

28. Richard D. Alexander, quoted by Francis Fukuyama, *The Great Disruption: Human Nature and the Reconstitution of Social Order* (New York: Free Press, 1999), 175.

29. Robert Hinde, *Bending the Rules: Morality in the Modern World— From Relationships to Politics and War* (Oxford: Oxford University Press, 2007), 154.

30. As Edward Carmines and James Stimson accurately note, "Citizens who choose to become active in electoral politics . . . do not merely become active in community affairs, they choose sides." Carmines and Stimson, *Race and the Transformation of American Politics,* 99.

31. Hinde, *Bending the Rules,* 156. The heavy moral element was also seen in the 2008 Democratic primary. As Democratic politicians chose sides, cries of "treason" were a frequent occurrence.

32. As Marc Hauser has stated, "Given our strong interest in helping the in-group and harming the out group, we now have the basis for large-scale cooperation among genetically unrelated individuals. This, together with our powerful systems of punishment, give us a solution to the paradox of human cooperation." Marc Hauser, *Moral Minds: How Nature Designed Our Universal Sense of Right and Wrong* (New York: HarperCollins, 2006), 417.

33. Robert Nozick, *The Examined Life: Philosophical Meditations* (New York: Simon & Schuster, 1989), 295–96. Nozick, who initially received attention for his conservative views in *Utopia, Anarchy, and the State* (New York: Basic Books, 1974), made significant centrist, even liberal, adjustments to his views in *The Examined Life.*

34. The extended best treatment of this thrust and parry that I have seen is by John Gilmour, *Strategic Disagreement* (Pittsburgh: University of Pittsburgh Press, 1995). The Nozick quotation also closely tracks the theory of issue evolution put forward by Carmines and Stimson.

35. Michael Kinsley, *Washington Post,* March 1, 2002.

36. David Frum, *Comeback: Conservatism That Can Win Again* (New York: Doubleday, 2008), 32.

37. John Hilley, *The Challenge of Legislation: Bipartisanship in a Partisan World* (Washington, D.C.: Brookings Institution Press, 2008), 229.

38. Ibid. Hilley has eloquently stated the practitioner's view, and in my view has the better of the argument with the critics. Not everyone is so sanguine about this political consensus. Eric Patashnik at the University of Virginia notes that political debates in America are con-

ducted against "the backdrop of a massive welfare, regulatory, and ad-
ministrative state in which everything the federal government does
has the support of the mass public or some important constituency.
The political and organizational inertia . . . means that it is increasingly
difficult for each party to alter the trajectory of domestic policy—
whether political polarization is relatively high or low." Eric Patashnik, "Polarization in Perspective: Comment on David Brady, John Fer-
ejohn, and Laurel Harbridge," in *Red and Blue Nation,* vol. 2, ed. Brady
and Nivola, 225.

39. One of the ironies of this process is that the better Congress
does its job of engaging on issues and resolving conflicting proposals,
the lower are its approval ratings. Robert Durr, John Gilmour, and
Christina Wolbrecht, "Explaining Congressional Approval," *American
Journal of Political Science* 41 (January 1997): 175–207. This conclusion,
when coupled with the fact that televising congressional proceedings
has also diminished approval ratings, leads to what I call the "legislators illusion." The harder Congress tries to do its job and the more it
seeks public approval, the worse its standing with the public. Fortunately, some of congressional leaders have been quite mature about
this dilemma. Nicholas Longworth, one of the ablest speakers of the
House, noted in 1929, well before the advent of television, that members of Congress "have been attacked, denounced, despised, hunted,
harried, blamed, looked-down upon, excoriated and flayed. I refuse to
take it personally." Quoted by Donald Wolfensberger, *Congress and the
People: Deliberative Democracy on Trial* (Baltimore: Johns Hopkins University Press, 2000), 283.

40. Gilmour notes that one of the major forces for party unifor-
mity is the discipline imposed by core constituencies on those who de-
viate from the party line. This risk is largely ignored by those who urge
elected officials to jump the traces of party discipline in the cause of
bipartisanship. E.g., in February 2008, the Maryland incumbent con-
gressmen Albert Wynn (Democrat) and Wayne Gilchrest (Republican)
were purged in party primaries for failing to heed their respective party
positions.

41. Party leaders would never be this explicit, but the 2008 campaign, which focused on the future of the Supreme Court and Senator Schumer's (D-N.Y.) quest for a "truly filibuster-free" Senate are
enough to establish intent. Senator Sheldon Whitehouse (D-R.I.)
came closest to stating the truth when he said that the with respect to
unified government, "I would rather own it and then have to perform
than continue with this back and forth with Republicans, particularly

when they are engaged in this determined policy of obstruct, obstruct, obstruct." *New York Times,* October 26, 2008. Although the intentions of the parties are clear, it is a separate matter as to whether a unified command of the federal establishment can not only be attained—the relatively easy part—but then maintained.

42. Jacob Cooke, ed., *The Federalist* (Middletown, Conn.: Wesleyan University Press, 1961), respectively, *Federalist 62,* 417; and *Federalist 51,* 349.

Chapter 7

1. Reconciliation can also be added to this list.

2. Gordon S. Wood, "An Affair of Honor," *New York Review of Books,* April 13, 2000, 67.

3. Sarah Binder and Steven Smith, *Politics or Principle? Filibustering in the United States Senate* (Washington, D.C.: Brookings Institution Press, 1997), 198.

4. Sarah Binder, *Stalemate: Causes and Consequences of Legislative Gridlock* (Washington, D.C.: Brookings Institution Press, 2003), 36–37. Binder derives the 50 percent number by creating a "numerator" for Mayhew's important bills. She creates a gridlock factor where Mayhew's important enacted legislation is the denominator and is divided by a numerator of all "salient issues." This lets her show what is left undone after the enactment of Mayhew's important laws are taken into account. Binder creates the numerator of salient issues from the *New York Times* editorial page. When I first read this, I hollered out to my wife to locate a nearby emergency defibrillator just in case it was needed as I kept reading. Upon calmer reflection, I believe the methodology has value.

5. Binder has a particular proposal of a descending number of votes—60, 57, 54, 51—needed to invoke cloture. Thus the minority would be given time to make their case, but the majority would be guaranteed a chance to pass their proposals with 51 votes at the end of the process. Although proposed as a middle-ground reform effort, many practitioners, including myself, see this as backdoor abolition of the filibuster. Binder and Steven Smith, *Politics or Principle?* 211.

6. The case for the constitutional options is made by Martin Gold, "The Constitutional Option to Change Senate Rules and Procedures," *Harvard Journal of Law and Public Policy* 28, no. 1 (2004): 205–72. Much of the commentary on the "constitutional option" has mixed two dis-

tinct issues. One is the wisdom of changing the cloture rule to a majority vote, and thus changing the nature of the Senate. The other is whether the precedents cited by proponents of the "constitutional option" are valid and thus would "work." Bob Dove, former parliamentarian in the Senate, has cut through the rhetorical flourishes with the following pithy analysis of the "constitutional option": "I'm against it, but it would certainly work." My own experience supports this view. When Senator Frist first began investigating the "constitutional option" in 2004, the Democratic staff response to me was not that it was invalid, but rather that their retaliation would be "nuclear" in kind.

7. Gregory Wawro and Eric Schikler, *Filibuster: Obstruction and Lawmaking in the U.S. Senate* (Princeton, N.J.: Princeton University Press, 2006), 3–4.

8. This could be called "when the worm turns" doctrine. See Avinah Dixit and Susan Skeath, *Games of Strategy* (New York: W. W. Norton, 1999), 93–97.

9. There is a solid intellectual case to be made for this observation. James Buchanan won a Nobel Prize in economics for his conclusion that private parties enter the political process seeking "profits" and that "logrolling" "appears as the very nature of the legislative process." James M. Buchanan and Gordon Tullock, *The Calculus of Consent: Logical Foundations of Constitutional Democracy* (Ann Arbor: University of Michigan Press, 1971), 5, 22. Given these risks, Buchanan concluded that supermajorities led to more "efficient results" and that simple majority voting would lead to "overinvestment" and waste in the public sector (pp. 143, 166, 301). This set of observations was given additional theoretical support by Marcur Olson, *The Rise and Decline of Nations: Economic Growth, Stagflation, and Social Rigidities* (New Haven, Conn.: Yale University Press, 1982), and entertaining anecdotal and literary support by Jonathan Rauch, *Demosclerosis: The Silent Killer of American Government* (New York: Random House, 1994).

10. *New York Times*, February 9, 2009.

11. John Hilley, *The Challenge of Legislation: Bipartisanship in a Partisan World* (Washington, D.C.: Brookings Institution Press, 2008).

12. Jacob Cooke, ed., *The Federalist* (Middletown, Conn.: Wesleyan University Press, 1961), *Federalist 51*, 349.

Index

Figures, notes, and tables are denoted by f, n, and t following the page number.